STORIES ETCHED IN MEMORIES

By Bill Clark

**Who I was: Sailor... Broadcaster... Chaplain
to Inmates, young and old!**

To Evelyn Olson

Bill Clark

My Teenage Prayer

*"Father, help me to spend my life
giving others a little BOOST up the Hill of
life!"*

Dear Andy:

Let me tell you about my growing up years, in reply to your request.
This will be a short book in itself.

Part 1
Growing Up

I was born in Los Angeles, California in 1927. My father was an airplane mechanic who worked for Howard Hughes, a world-famous designer and builder of airplanes.

Dad was a womanizer and an alcoholic. The "legacy" he left me is painful, in that he kept a mental record of all of his sexual conquests, even up to his death at age 73. I will not tell you the exact number that he bragged about.

My mother died when I was only two years old. After her death, I was sent to central California to be raised by an aunt and uncle. They had no children of their own, so they became Mom and Dad to me.

It was 1929, the time of the world-wide Depression. Television had not been invented yet, nor FM radio... no computers... no music on CD... no cell phones... no airplanes able to fly around the world in a matter of hours. You name it...compared to the present technology, *life was ancient!*

There was one positive thing, however; <u>we had never heard of drugs!</u>

I was raised on a small farm of only 10 acres. My folks raised several thousand chickens regularly, and had an almond orchard. My daily chores after school each afternoon included was to gathering eggs, putting them in egg crates in a cool cellar, and then bury any hens who might have died.

We did not have any modern plumbing. Our only resource was a single hole outhouse.

I also did not have a bedroom of my own. We did have a small barn, which became my bedroom. Dad built a platform about 4 inches above the dirt floor, and put my bed on top of it. In summer we had hordes of mosquitos, so to keep them from eating me alive, I draped a netting over the bed and let'em buzz all they wanted.

The kids in the area all had summer jobs working in peach orchards and grape vineyards. Our wages were only 20 cents per hour, and it was hot sweaty work. The peach fuzz made us itch like crazy. After work, I had no shower, so my only solution was to take a bar of soap and jump into the irrigation ditch in front of our house. Sometimes my buddies would come by in an old jalopy pickup truck. We'd take our 22 rifles and shotguns out into the alfalfa fields to hunt jack rabbits.

On weekends those buddies came by again, and we'd head for a river about 4 miles away, to go fishing. When the fish stopped biting, we'd go skinny-dipping. We'd climb up into trees with lone vines, grab one, swing out over the water like Tarzan of the Apes would do, let go, and drop down naked into the river! It was great fun for guys. Sometimes we'd choose up teams and hide out among the trees, playing Cowboys vs. Indians. We also threw dirt clods at each other. If a nearby field had watermelons growing in it, we'd sneak out and steal a few melons. Now I feel guilty about the stealing, but farmers knew we were farm boys and never complained. When we ate our fill, we would enjoy spitting seeds at each other, and have a contest to see who could spit seeds the farthest.

Travel? In those days our parents' car would only go about 40 miles per hour, and there were only two lane roads. There were no yellow lines down the center, or white lines along the sides. Also, car rear doors opened forwards, rather than backward. That caused many dangerous accidents, if someone opened a rear door while the car was moving.

As far as our social life, we lived out in the country, and most of the teens did okay. However, a few of them did "make out" in the back seat of a car, as hormones were active in even those days. Me? I only had a bicycle and strong moral standards!

Our little Sunday School was held in a small three room school house. We normally did not have any guest speakers. However, one Sunday we had a special guest. He was only 19 years old; a handsome young guy, who just dazzled all of us with his talent. He played the trombone, told stories, and sang with a tremendous Baritone Voice. It was his music and dynamic personality that persuaded me to make my decision to ask Jesus into my heart! *If I were to tell you his name, you would probably recognize him, because in only a few months he began a Life Changing career!* (Including my own.)

One of the songs he sang was called, **"Ship ahoy!"** He also told a moving story of two sailing ships from past generations. First, a bad storm had damaged the primary sailing vessel to the point where all of the Life Boats had been destroyed or swept overboard. Second, another sailing ship engaged in battle with it, and both ships were shooting cannon balls at one another!

The main vessel took a cannon ball hit at the water line, and ocean water began to pour into it. The situation was so critical that the Ship's Captain called, **"All Hands On Deck!"** He continued, *"Men, you know we are sinking fast. But there is <u>one</u> possibility the ship can be saved! However, for this to happen, one of you <u>will have to give up his own life to save the rest of us!</u>*

I'm going to turn my back and ask for a volunteer to step forward to dive overboard, and wedge himself into that shell hole to stop water from coming in. Then we'll stuff mattresses around him and the rest of our crew can be saved!

When the Captain turned his back and asked for a volunteer to step forward, the one who did so, was the Captain's own SON!

"Oh Son... not you!" said the Captain. The son replied, *"Father, I love my shipmates. These men have families at home. And you said <u>anyone!</u>"*

Finally the Captain agreed. So the men lined up to hug and shake hands with the son, and told the boy how grateful they were, and they'd never forget him, etc. So, the deed was done, and the ship and its crew made it home safely.

<u>Listening to this awesome story moved me to personally ask Jesus into my own heart! And from that moment, my own life has been spent loving and serving Jesus!</u>

It was only a few months after this incident at our Sunday school that this young singer/story teller, met and joined with another young man who wanted to bring the Gospel to others.

The two men formed an Evangelistic Association, and held their very *first* Crusade in nearby Modesto, California.

You know these two men as Billy Graham, and his song leader <u>Cliff Barrows!</u>

"Summer Camp!"

Each summer it was the custom of the American Sunday School Union to host camps for young people. We were not affiliated with any particular church, but instead were from small communities, mostly outside of towns or cities.

One year when I was about 17, a number of kids from central California were bussed to Santa Rosa, a mountainous region north of San Francisco, not far from the Napa Valley Wine country. There, we joined other youth for a couple of weeks camping out, and we were rather "roughing it" in that there were no cabins, kitchens or covered buildings. Instead, we did have picnic tables, and we unrolled our sleeping bags under trees. I cannot recall where our food came from, but there were adults who planned details, and led good times and spiritual sessions.

We experienced two times which were to us, nothing short of miraculous. The first event had to do with keeping us from being rained on. We received word from Forest Rangers that a storm was headed our way, and we should prepare for buckets of rain falling on us one evening. Our Superintendent said, *"Let's Pray about it!"* So we did! That night, rain did in fact fall; <u>all around us,</u> like in a circle. But not a single drop fell on our camp! God had answered our prayer, in a way beyond our expectations!

Protection #2

It must have been a day later that we were all having breakfast. Suddenly we heard the sound of airplane engines (this is during WWII). We heard two planes. Then, one of the planes began a steep dive, getting louder and louder, and getting closer and closer to us... then SUDDENLY THE SOUND STOPPED! There is NO way I can describe how quickly the screaming dive ended!

I do not recall why a few of us boys decided to take an afternoon hike through the forest, nor why we picked a certain direction to walk. But when we walked out into a clearing, *<u>we were stunned!</u>* There were the remains of a P-38 Twin Engine fighter plane. Smoke still rising from the debris. Of course we had to investigate! We found body remains, small but certainly human. The largest parts of that plane were the two engine blocks, each 3 or 4 feet long. All other fragments were small and numerous. We all sat down in shock, and prayed silently, remembering how loudly the roar of that Fighter Plane became, only to end in a nanosecond!

It was time to return to camp and attempt to describe the carnage and the death of a brave pilot!

If that plane had crashed in our camp, all of us would have been killed!

Thank you Father for protecting your children!

High School Days:

All of us kids rode buses 4 miles to school each day. In High School, there were only 133 students in the entire school. We didn't have a lot of activities, so our school spirit was low, and the kids were bored. I wanted to do something about it, so I ran for Student Body President... and I won, and I came up with a lot of activities. We purchased a Juke Box Record player for noontime dances, and a Movie Projector with a built-in speaker, which doubled as a Loud Speaker.

The biggest problem was ME! I got a big head, and I was on an ego trip. It wasn't until <u>after</u> graduation that I learned I had turned a lot of kids off, and it was too late to make amends.

In retrospect, that pride at the time was a lesson well learned. Later on in life, God helped me to keep that ego in check! (Remember – Pride is what got Satan and his followers thrown out of Heaven.)

Military Days!

WWII was winding down, but I was about to turn 18, and I needed to make a decision: Wait to be drafted, or join the Military! I chose to join the Navy, and left for Boot Camp in San Diego just two days after graduating high school.

No matter which branch of service you are in, the goal of boot camp staff is: (1) To break every recruit down in order to change all personal self ego and independence away. (2) And then rebuild that man into a person who learns to place his <u>team,</u> it's safety, and purpose <u>first!</u> I counsel teen-age boys today that **Military Boot Camp will make a Man of you!**

I was in Navy Boot Camp in mid summer of 1945 when US Bombers dropped Atomic Bombs on Japan, and the Nipponese finally surrendered! After completing boot camp I was sent overseas to the Pacific arena, and landed in the Philippine Islands on December 7, 1945... *just 4 years to the day after Pearl Harbor was bombed!*

Years later I had the opportunity of interviewing the Japanese pilot who led the attack on Pearl harbor. Captain Mitsuo Fuchida later became a Christian and a

Missionary to his own people and the United States! He even preached in a Klamath Falls, Oregon church.

My first assignment in the Philippines was on a Navy LCI (Landing Craft Infantry). Since the war had ended and many Radiomen were being sent home, it gave me the opportunity to strike (or learn) to become a Radio Operator. I already knew Morse code, but my skills were not developed yet for copying dots and dashes at a high speed. Most messages were at about 18 words per minute. Encoded secret messages were difficult, since missing a single letter nullified that message.

Bill copying Morse Code

The Islands

LCI's were like a small yacht, but designed to

run up on a beachhead and drop off troops during an invasion (Now past). Our duty at that time was to take people or equipment to southern islands. That gave me the opportunity to see many of the 7,086 Philippine islands, some only the size of large rocks sticking above the water.

Seeing History

One of those islands was the home of Cebu City, a major city where our military was stationed during WWII. I had heard that the famous Spanish Explorer, Ferdinand Magellan, had visited a small island nearby, so I made exploring that site a "must see" for me.

Centuries past, Magellan had come ashore at the tip of a long, but very pristine, island. At that spot, a Filipino warrior named *Lapoo Lapoo* took his spear and killed the explorer! To us visitors, all we saw was a normal sandy beach.

However, nearby was a 15' tall memorial spike where Japanese soldiers had crudely painted, **"This is what happens to enemies of Japan!"**

In personal retrospect, even today, of all of the places I have visited in the world, this memorial stands out the most! Very few people even <u>know</u> about, let alone visit it! *Thank you*

Lord!

Typhoon Survival

During the summer of 1946, I was a US Navy radio operator, assigned to Weather Patrol duty in the Philippine Islands. Our task was to proceed 200 miles off the Philippine eastern coast, and to report weather conditions to Naval Headquarters for about 3 weeks at a time.

Typhoons usually originate in that region, especially in summer months. Our ship would navigate to a specified area of approximately a 20 mile circle. If the weather was calm and waves were fairly smooth we would shut off the ship's engines, and only restart them when we drifted outside that geographical circle.

Periodically, we would release a Weather Balloon (about 3' in size) and let it drift upwards. However the balloon had a small radio transmitter attached to it, and our Aerographer's Mate (weather man) would give me the data, and I in turn would send a Morse Code message to shore. I sent those messages every 4 hours daily. During other specified hours, I listened to Fox reports. Fox meant general information all ships at sea needed to know. **But during those sessions, I**

specifically listened for our own ship's Call Sign for any message addressed specifically to us alone.

I spent 2 years on this ship while in China

Our ship was the PCE885... (Patrol Craft Escort) which was about half the size of a small Destroyer Escort. I spent over a year on the 885. There were 2 other PCE's who rotated with us for those 3 week assignments.

This was my Weather Patrol Ship, the PCE 885

When typhoons generated on our site, or traveled through our vicinity, we were at the mercy of strong winds and perilous 75' high wave troughs. One minute we were on top of a mountain of turbulent ocean. Seconds later, our ship was a like a toy heading downward, and we prayed desperately that the Helmsman could keep our bow headed straight down, directly into the unyielding turbulence. Were he unable to keep that heading, it would mean disaster for ship and crew. We were but a helpless speck of steel. It seemed like time stood still, and we held our breath. Did 1 say STILL? Nothing stood still... absolutely nothing! There was continuous rolling, twisting, jarring and uncertainty!

On one occasion, we had been at our Duty Station for about three weeks, and it was time for us to be relieved by another PCE. Instead of a PCE, we were replaced for the first time by a much smaller vessel... a PGM (Patrol Gun Boat). The PGM is what the name implies... a Boat, only meant to be used for navigating rivers. It had a small, inexperienced crew, and sported only a single bow gun. I don't remember the caliber of the gun... but I do recall that it's shells were about 18" long.

This boat did not have a Radio Operator, so I was given orders to go aboard that small boat, and send in the necessary weather data. How was I supposed to get aboard? Just jump over! Because the boat was several feet below our main deck level, the PGM came within only a few feet along side of us. I tossed my Sleeping bag over, and Jumped! Waiting sailors grabbed us both.

Little did I know what the next several weeks would become, especially for me...it's "Radioman". My very own life turned out to be a key element in the safety of every sailor, officer, and the boat itself.

The vessel had a very small superstructure! (The Bridge, where Commanding Officer, and Helmsman were stationed.) My mental calculations of the Boats' length was about 45' long, and 14' wide. Out front, the Bow gun aimed forward, slightly elevated. In the event of heavy seas, that Bow gun took the brunt of all the massive waves, plus the added weight of the entire boat when we were heading downward into a huge trough of ocean!

This is the PGM (Patrol Gun Boat) which almost capsized.

None of us aboard were aware of the frightening hours ahead of us, when that bow would be tested beyond limits.

The Radio Shack was just below the Bridge, at main deck level. Heading aft toward the fantail everything was flat, except for an entrance to the Chow Hall. I'm guessing there was about 15 feet from the exit of the radio shack and the fantail. Four Diesel engines were below!

(More about them later.)

Before going any further in this story, let me explain the makeup of a Typhoon: The next time you flush water down a sink, notice the water drains in a clockwise flow, cut into four sections. The top right drainage is small, then water dropping into the lower right quarter has a larger flow toward the bottom. Bottom left flow is very strong, but lessens moving up to the top left quarter. However, the center of a Typhoon is called The Eye, and is less turbulent until you re-enter another quadrant.

Now back to the first two uneventful weeks!
One afternoon, several of the PGM crewmen were leaning against a side rail, bitching and complaining about the monotony of little activity. As I walked by, one of the sailors stopped me and asked, "Clark, how long have you been on sea duty?" I counted the weeks on my fingers and said, "This trip? Lets see, this is my fifth week!" The men shook their heads and shut up. No more gripes!

Back to the Radio Shack: My space was the width of a metal desk. On a shelf above was a Radio Receiver barely within reach. The receiver was fairly large, and was supposed to be held in place by a bolt under each corner. The receiver must have weighed about 35 pounds. Below the radio was a small drawer about 4 inches tall. Then came my desk, a typewriter, and a small transmitter top right. In rough weather, I had to grasp the left desk side, and use my right hand to tap out (send) messages with a Morse Code Key. A key is only 2 ½" wide, 1 ½" high, and a 5" curved metal bar with a plastic knob at the end closest to it's operator. Springs allow a radioman to adjust a key to whatever speed he is comfortable with, while sending the dots & dashes of Morse code.

About three weeks into our mission, there was a sudden change in weather conditions! Bear in mind that Typhoons travel at wind speeds exceeding 100 knots. Sometimes a typhoon originates at your location, and at other times, it may just bear across your path. In our case, I had not received any radio messages about one approaching us. Apparently it formed rapidly in our area. Dark skies descended on us, and strong waves gripped us. Winds howled loudly. Our little boat was tossed & turned like a toy!

In the radio shack, I wore headphones, and listened frantically for any incoming messages. All I heard was static and loud clashes of thunderous noise. I hung on to the nearest object within reach. Our Boat rolled from one side to the other. Up... down... sideways... tremendous noise crashes everywhere... banging sounds all over, as the Captain and Helmsman struggled to keep us afloat. I was glued to my earphones vainly listening for orders from shore to change course. No message!

The little vessel just shook, rolled one way, then another way... up... down... jarring... banging! Objects in the shack slid by my feet. This was getting Scary! How long the chaos went on, I do not know... it just seemed endless!

Then all of a sudden the ship took a huge 65 degree roll to Starboard!

The best way I can describe it is: it felt like our boat had been flushed down the toilet.

How do I know it was 65 degrees? A quick look up! There was a free swinging, single arm gauge with large numbers clearly indicating every degree.

Other things happened too. That little drawer below my radio receiver flew out over me and hit the Aerographer Mate behind me in the head! He looked up just in time to see and catch the heavy radio receiver, which was about to fall on me. It was only then that we realized the receiver was just bolted down by two front bolts, but NOT at all four corners! Had this man not caught the receiver, I could have been seriously injured!

Damage control:

Ammunition in storage only a few feet in front of my office, broke loose and began to slam back and forth from one bulkhead to the other. Those shells got hot, and were in danger of exploding. Skipper ordered overhead water sprinklers turned on to cool the ammo. Then, after the shells cooled off, crewmen were ordered inside to grab those large shells and toss them overboard. If you've ever been in rough seas, you know how difficult it is just to stand upright, let alone carry a heavy object. It was dangerous for the sailors who risked being injured or swept overboard. Drainage water from the overhead sprinkler system seeped down into the crew's quarters below deck, and eventually drained down to the engine room and Bilge pumps.

Moving aft, other than the big roll, the Cook in the rear galley was unaware of forward damage. He just wanted out of there, and hung on to a rope to keep from being swept overboard. Upon entering my office, the cook

looked down into the crews' quarters, and saw a foot of water. I've never seen a man so scared! With eyes the size of saucers he squeaked out: "Ah...Claaark! You gonna... aah... send out aah... an SOS?' I said, 'No! Why?' 'We're sinkin' ain't we?' he said. To which I replied, 'Thank God not quite!'"
Apparently we had passed through the first turbulence, directly into the Eye of the storm. Wind was less strong, and waves were smaller. We had not anticipated finding ourselves there!

But guess what... **we still had another quarter to pass thru**.

I was still glued to my headphones.... straining to hear through all the chaos of atmospheric noises...seeking to pickup ANY signal sent to us, we were incapable of calling anyone! To this very day I struggle with questions of my part on that hellish day. Was I supposed to have heard a signal directing us to change course but missed it? Was it MY fault?

Somehow we made it through the quieter eye of the storm, then out the final segment of rocking, rolling, falling, bouncing, and outright misery.

Returning Home

After the typhoon had passed, it took us two slow days to return to base. Seawater had mixed into our diesel fuel; four of our diesel injectors (spark plugs) were not operating correctly. We were only capable of a few knots speed. When we looked over the sides, and the boat took a normal rolling side movement we could see water squirting out from the engine room. No wonder...those faithful engines had put up a good fight! I'd like to think... we all did!

Then we returned to our base and the PCE 885. One afternoon, I decided to visit a basketball court where Sailors and Marines were shooting baskets. One Marine was talking to his buddies. He had a patch on his face, but he looked familiar. Finally it hit me like a ton of bricks, **"That's my cousin Les!"** I came up to him, grinning from ear to ear, tapped him on the shoulder and called him by a nickname only he and I knew... **"Hi Doc!"** Can you imagine the odds against anything like this happening? *Here we were 7,000 miles from home and I run into my own cousin!*

Reflections

I'm a firm believer that absolutely <u>nothing</u>

<u>happens by accident</u> in the lives of God's children. I suspect many of the PGM's crew may have learned to pray sincerely, for the *first time* in their lives.

Only the Lord knows what changes that Typhoon may have made in their lives. Praise The Lord!

Rescue At Sea!

After about 18 months aboard the weather patrol craft PCE 885, it was long past time for all of us aboard ship to head back State side and home!

We left the Philippine Islands and headed toward Guam. Boy were we glad! It was to be a slow trip however, because we were to be the lead ship in a flotilla of two other slow vessels. We had to poke along at a much slower speed than a PCE was capable of travelling. One of them was a small Army Cargo ship, and the other was a large Navy LST (Landing Ship Tank.)

One clear day, one of our Lookouts reported seeing what appeared to be a lifeboat off of our starboard side. Altering course, there was indeed a lifeboat. We saw 17 native people crowded into a small boat, less than 16' long. As we approached, the natives saw our large 3" deck gun, which they immediately recognized as a war vessel and made them afraid. However, they barely had enough strength to raise their arms, and we immediately realized they needed help!

Skipper ordered a cargo net to be lowered over the side, while husky sailors climbed down to assist the helpless victims. Other sailors ran below decks to retrieve mattresses for the natives to lay on.

One of the natives was a woman, carrying a small girl about 2 years old. It was apparent that the woman had attempted to breast feed her child, but had no milk to nurture the little girl. Her breasts were hot, and she continually poured the cold water over herself, which we provided to reduce her temperature. We quickly provided food, but attempted to caution them to eat slowly, and in only small amounts.

Communication was slow, because none of them spoke English. They Wore crosses around their necks, held them up, pointed to the sky and then to us, signifying we were the answer to their prayers.

Using Orange peels and drawing pictures we were able to piece their story together in this manner: they were natives of the Samoan Islands, on route somewhere in a sailboat. Apparently rough seas and strong winds capsized their boat, and originally 19 people squeezed into this small lifeboat we found them in. An old man and a child had died during 21 days of struggle, and the two were thrown overboard. That explained to us why the water under their boat was black, and churning with thousands of Prauhna, a deadly fish that can shred meat from bones in seconds. The fish were waiting for more bodies.

We signaled the Army ship to use their Cargo Boom to pickup the lifeboat, but it broke in half and sank. Their crewmen told us that just one more large wave would have destroyed the boat. Our natives saw the breakup and were dismayed, because all of their remaining possessions were now lost.

Back on board our ship what impressed me was that the hardest old salty sailors on our ship were the most tender and loving crewmen in aiding the native survivors... especially to the two year old baby girl. These men spent hours on end combing her blond hair and treated her like a princess.

Since I was the Radio Operator, my assistance was to notify shore bases that we had rescued 17 survivors. I long remember the thrill it gave me to announce to "all ships at sea" and any other listening ear, the story of how we had rescued helpless natives who had been adrift at sea for 21 horrendous days.

We were diverted south to the Pelau Islands to deliver our Samoan natives ashore. Since they had now no possessions at all, our crewmen took up a collection of about $200 cash to give them.

What a joy it was to see those thankful native faces and hands reaching out to us in fond and grateful farewell for saving their lives!

China Duty

After two years in the Philippines, and a 30 day leave at home, I was sent back overseas again, this time to China, in August of 1947.

Our troop ship took us to the north China coast city of Tsingtao! (pronounced Chingdow). Before we had our first Liberty ashore, we were warned: Do not go ashore alone, plus some other cautions. We learned right away to be assertive. So when we stepped foot off base and rickshaw drivers started to grab and pull us into his own rickshaw, we brushed their hands off us, and acted unafraid!

Tsingtao was an old German built city from past occupation. The buildings were well built, with red tile roofs. Rickshaws and bicycles were everywhere, by the thousands!

There were NO cars! For that matter...no paved streets...only cobblestones (large uniform sized rocks). However, on each side of the street were smooth stones about a foot wide, in a continuous, unbroken row. Coolies pulled fully loaded wooden wheeled ox carts on those rows. Over many years, the stones had been worn into a rut. The problem: Those grooved stones did not curve to the left or right at intersections. Thus, the coolies had to seesaw back and forth until the cart was in another groove. One day I watched them make vain attempts to get back on grooved stones, but to no avail. I went over, and used one arm to exert leverage, immediately freeing the cart. The coolies were amazed, and thought I was a superman. They had never learned the simple law of leverage! How ancient? ...mid summer 1947.

China, at that period, was led by Generalissimo Chiang Ki Shek, from his headquarters in Nanking, on the shores of the Yangtze River. His people were struggling to survive. For us sailors we saw how difficult life was! We were hounded by beggars pleading *"Cumsha, Joe.Cumsha!"* The most heart breaking were the Lepers! It was horrible to see what was once a human being, now only a semblance of life, dragging itself along the ground, eyes now in sockets, teeth gone, ears gone, the face of a skull barely covered by pockmarked skin. Only the stub of an arm or leg remained, with perhaps a single hand extended... begging, pleading, filthy rags were all that was left of what was once clothing. Always those piercing, empty pleas, *"Cumsha, Joe!"* It broke our hearts! A million dollar gift would not have changed their condition! We had no choice but to walk on by and agonize over their fate!

Inflation Beyond Belief!

When we first landed in China, the ratio of Chinese money to ours was about $1,000 CNC (Chinese National Currency) to $1 U.S. But every day, even hourly, their inflation sky rocketed. Their bills were printed in terms of $10,000 each. One day in Shanghai I walked past a car with two men in the back seat, who were literally up to their necks in bundles of money! Officials tried one plan after another to stem the tide of inflation, all unsuccessfully! About a year after our arrival in China, several of us sailors were sent north for a week's vacation in Peking (now Beijing.) One evening at a single meal, I actually spent $12,000! That was only $1 American. I still remember what the meal was: fresh milk and fried frog's legs!

Solution...

Money was changed to Gold Yuan, at a ration of $7 Yuan to $1 US. However, the penalty was death for anyone caught using U.S. dollars. Even we GI's were paid in Yuan. Today, Yuan is still the currency in China, with freedom to use American dollars.

"The Rest of The Story"
An Epic of the HMS Black Swan

Famed Radio Broadcaster Paul Harvey hosted a weekly narrative called "The Rest Of the Story!" The following is my own delayed event...

I was a participant and observer to an event, which took place in China during 1948.
However, it took 30 years before I knew the conclusion of a traumatic war situation. As background, let me explain that this story took place during the beginning of Chinese Communist General Mao Dze Dung's conquest of China. Generalisimo Chiang Kai Shek was Emperor of the land. His palace was located along the banks of the mighty Yangtze River, until Chairman Mao deposed him. Mao's strategy to conquer was to surround small cities while recruiting his army and gaining strength. In effect, he cut off and isolated portions of mainland China over several years.

The LSM-444 I was on for 2 years in China.

The US Navy had a base on the north coast city of Tsing-Tao, (pronounced Ching dao.)

I was a radio operator there aboard the LSM-444, a flat-bottomed amphibious craft designed to carry tanks, trucks and equipment for beach landings during wartime.

With us were several larger vessels, a Hospital Ship and a couple of Destroyers in our unit. Our real reason for being in China at all was to aid in the evacuation of U.S. and

foreign national citizens, if and when Mao made his move to take over China.

Touchy Rescue!

Mao's forces had Tsing-Tao surrounded within 25 miles for almost two years during our stay. Let me tell you about an event in which two intoxicated US Marines wandered outside the city limits and were captured by Communist forces: In order to rescue our Marines the LSM-444 was assigned the task of approaching a stretch of Chinese shoreline, and aid in negotiations for their release. Our shallow bottom permitted us to move to within several hundred yards of shore, drop anchor, make observations and await a negotiating team to arrive to request the return of the two men.

Our Captain watched the shore with binoculars for any signs of activity, then relayed what he saw to me in the Radio Shack, and I in turn would send radio messages to my senior ship on the horizon. Skipper told me to report that there were only a few Equine on shore, plus a hay stack. I asked him, "Sir what's an Equine?" (I'd never heard a Horse called an equine). Then when a US Destroyer arrived on the scene, the haystack suddenly turned around, and a large gun barrel was aimed directly at us on the LSM-444!

Our own crews took sight on the haystack, and

I had the uncomfortable feeling that a shell might come flying through my radio shack at any moment. Fortunately, no one squeezed a trigger. Eventually a small boat came in from the Destroyer, passed by us enroute to shore, and after several days, the US Marines were released.

China Travels

It was not uncommon for us to conduct military maneuvers off the coast of Tsing Dao, which I assume were meant to show our presence. We also traveled south to Shanghai on several occasions. I recall meeting Southern Baptist Missionaries in a church in that huge city, and several of us Christian sailors were invited to their home for Sunday dinner. Those people became loving friends, who taught us how to eat with chopsticks, helped us understand China better, and made us lonely sailors feel at home away from home.

Mao Makes His Move! Navy officials, realizing that all out war was imminent, gave LSM-444 orders to leave Shanghai and travel 200 miles up the Yangtze River to Nanking. Upon arrival, we picked up several dozen missionaries, and civilians of foreign countries, and then took them down river to safety in Shanghai. We had no idea we were being closely watched by Communist eyes following our progress down the Yangtze. Arriving back at Shanghai, our ship was loaded with Aircraft Ground Approach trucks and equipment. We were given orders to sail to Formosa, (today's Taiwan), and then proceed back to the US. Shanghai's waterfront is located on a small river, which is a tributary of the Yangtze. We started to leave the Wangpoo tributary back into the Yangtze, when we received orders to return to meet some British ships.

War View!

Back at the waterfront we were thunderstruck by seeing two badly damaged warships awaiting us. Three British Warships had been ambushed by Communist forces in the locations we had only recently sailed, unaware of any danger. Only hours following our trip, the British light cruiser *HMS London*, and two frigates *Amethyst*, and *Black Swan* were attacked by Communist forces. Heavy artillery had been positioned closely along riverbanks for a surprise attack. The *London* and *Amethist* sustained heavy damages, but managed to escape. Meanwhile, the Black Swan was trapped and helpless. The communists wanted to capture the Frigate intact. If the ship moved, or returned fire, it was hit by deadly shore guns. A virtual surrender of the vessel was demanded. How that scenario played out is another story all it's own.

British Wounded!

Meanwhile, back in Shanghai, we saw pain and shell shock! Huge holes pockmarked the Cruiser and Frigate. There was a hushed silence, as wounded sailors were placed on stretchers and handed down to our own crew for transport to the US Hospital ship Repose. I'll never forget the pitiful sight of a British officer who had a large hole in his back. He died while his stretcher was handed over to our crewmen. Our mercy mission was done, and we had to leave China for good. After we left, 1 some how heard rumors that the Black Swan had made it to safety.

Fast Forward!

Thirty years later, as a faculty member of Oregon Institute of Technology, in Klamath Falls, I was invited to recruit students from The Dalles High School located near the Columbia River. At the end of the day, each college representative retired to his or her motel room for the night. For some reason, I was restless and could not sleep, so I decided to see what was on TV. I tuned into a black and white movie in progress, where two British sailors were talking. One of them said something about... *the Black Swan!* Those words triggered my memory, and I thought... *"Black Swan?" Why does that sound familiar? Oh yes, I remember now! That was the British Frigate trapped on the Yangtze! "*

I was hooked! For nearly an hour I heard what actually happened those many years ago. Incredibly, one of the sailors mentioned, " *A US Navy LSM is on it's way!"* I shouted out loud, *"That was us!"* Wow!

Here's what happened: The Frigate's officers refused to surrender their vessel! Finally after two days of negotiations, with fuel and food supplies dwindling, the Brits decided on a daring plan of escape. Under cover of darkness they strung a line from the stern of the vessel up to the mast, then down to the bow. Over that line they draped dark canvas, to make the ship's super structure appear much larger than it actually was. Their reasoning was that when the communists saw that large hulk moving in the dark down stream, the gunfire would be targeted above the vessel and do no damage. It worked! Traveling down stream at flank speed, the Black Swan had only one area illuminated by a search light, and continued to safety.

I was cheering at the top of my voice! *"So that's what happened!"* Life is amazing! After thirty years... as Paul Harvey would say: "**And now you know**... *the rest of the story.*"

EPILOGUE

Scripture asserts that God controls even the rulers of nations whose plans and devices are evil. God even uses them for His own purposes. In Isaiah 55:8 He says, "My ways are not your Ways. "

Communist leader Mao Dze Dung was a ruthless dictator who murdered thousands of Chinese people and enslaved them into atheism.

However some of Mao's policies God turned into positives. Two of his decisions have resulted in amazing transformations to China which only in recent years, have become apparent.

1. The alphabet and language were simplified to make reading and education more practical. From a spiritual standpoint, literally millions of Chinese become Christians each year, in spite of government oppression. Today in Nanking China, Amity Press prints millions of Chinese Bibles yearly. Yet those Bibles fall short of reaching the 1.3 billion plus population. Millions of Christians have yet to own a single copy of the Bible, and long to own one. Some of us have had the privilege in recent years to travel back to China and place a Bible in eager hands. The people are ecstatic,

and thankful beyond imagination. It is like placing a million dollar gift in their hands. They hug us, radiate joy, sing, clap their hands, and repeat, *"Shang dee JuPo Nee!"* God Bless you!

What a humbling and gratifying experience.

2. Another achievement of Mao Dze Dung was revolutionizing transportation. Today there are millions of automobiles traveling four lane highways from southern China to

the northern borders. The result not only has spurred the economy, but permits the Gospel to be transported nationwide in a matter of hours. Our group alone, dispersed over 6,000 Bibles in this manner.

"SAILOR To PREACHER"

I spent almost two years in China. Then just before leaving for the States, the Lord started to deal with me about the future. One morning at my duty station in the Radio Shack, I was using a bucket of water to wash the bulkheads (walls). In my mind, the Lord asked me, "Bill, you're getting out of the Navy in about two months. What are you going to do with your life? Would you be willing to serve me?" At first I hesitated. But I had walked with the Lord most of my life, and realized that to not obey Him would mean a miserable and empty life. So I answered: "Okay Lord, but you'll have to show me what to do, and how to do it!" Little did I realize that my commitment to God's Calling would lead to amazing, lifelong adventures **full of purpose**, for the rest of my life!

God's leading was specific and incredible!

Back home, I enrolled in Junior College Radio Broadcasting courses. Then one day I was asked to speak in a church. After that very first sermon, the church members asked me to take the place of their pastor who was retiring in several months. I was amazed that they would consider an inexperienced 23 year old to be their pastor. After much prayer and persuasion from other pastors, I stepped out on faith to lead the church. One of my college classmates was Jack Brooks, who helped out as our Sunday School Superintendent.

We both graduated from Junior College in two years. Jack had planned to continue toward a four year degree in Radio Engineering at Fresno State. I sensed a need to enroll in a Bible college, but had no college in mind.

God had plans neither of us knew about!

During summer vacation Jack and I took teenagers from our church on a camping trip to the hills. One afternoon Jack was at the top of a hill where our sleeping bags were rolled out. I was at the bottom of that hill, about 100 yards away, sitting on a log in the fire pit area. Mentally, not aloud, I asked the Lord: "Do you want me to attend a Bible College? Where?" There was no audible voice. But into my mind came words slowly, gently, and specifically: "I want you and Jack to go to Pacific Bible College, and prepare to serve Me in Christian Broadcasting." I shook my head in shock and thought "What was that?" Then I jumped up and went running up the hill to see Jack! Arriving there all out of breath, I panted, *"Jack, I want to talk to you!"* He just grinned at me, and said "Sit down, I know what you're gonna say!" To which I replied, "What do you mean... you know what I'm gonna say?" Jack replied, "Did the Lord speak to you a couple of minutes ago?" I paused, "yyyyyYes. How did you know?" "He spoke to me too! Lets write down on notes what the Lord told each one of us!" The notes were identical!

The two of us went off to PBC, were roommates, and graduated with Bachelor Degrees in Bible! He later spent about 40 years as a Missionary Radio Engineer, with Far East Broadcasting.

Flying Lessons

When my friend Jack Brooks and I were enrolled at Pacific Bible College, we became interested in the work of Jungle Aviation & Radio Service Missions!

So we drove to a small airport about 20 miles from campus called **Brackets Field!**
We were given the opportunity to work for our flight time by gassing planes, and helping in a hanger to repair small planes. The plan was that we were given the equivalent of $1 per hour of work which counted toward one hour of Flight Training.

We were hooked! At that time it took 40 hours of written exams and flight training. We each soloed in about 8 hours. The small plane we flew in was a Piper Pacer, side by side. (Pilot and student next to each other.)

One of the slightly dangerous features of the Pacer was that it had no self -starting engine. It was necessary for Jack or I to exchange taking hold of the Propeller out front, listen for count down from pilot… then swiftly pull the prop down and step back hurriedly! If the plane didn't start, then we repeated the process.

The Piper Pacer also was a *"Tail Dragger,"*

which meant the plane had to pick up enough speed for the tail to raise rather than be drug. Meantime, the pilot had to use rudder pedals left or right alternately to keep the flight path straight ahead. As airspeed increased, his foot pedal distance became shorter, until take off. It was exciting!

Today, tail-draggers have been replaced with fixed rolling Nose Gear!

Jack was the first of us to solo, and also to take his Cross Country solo flight.

Our instructor named Steve, was a very quiet man. We heard that he felt what we would call today PTSD, (Post Traumatic Stress Disorder," from the many flights he took during WWII on flights from the Himalayas, Burma, and India to China deliveries.

On one training exercise, Steve allowed me to fly to busy Los Angeles International Airport. It was also the time I flew a high winged Super Family Cruiser model. He did tell me this plane had lift that *made it want to keep on flying*, while I anticipated it would land.

My Own Plane!

Surplus airplanes were a dime a dozen. One of them was a PTl9, low wing Open Cockpit Trainer. It was sitting all alone in a separate part of the airport, where it was parked by a man who gave up flying. Why? There was so much smog over much of Southern California that it would bring tears to the eyes of everyone. (In fact, when Jack & I travelled by car, one person would gauge our location via map, and give the driver instructions of where to turn.) The PTl9's owner almost didn't make it back to the landing field alive because of the smog. I was told the owner would take only $100.

College loans or not, **l had to own that plane**! **MY** Plane… had an in-line Lycoming
Engine, about 2' long for just the engine block itself. There were bird nests that I had to clean & clear out first. Eventually I got **MY** plane's engine started, and had a ball *TAXIING* down the runway, as proud as could be.

Next came the task of trying to get it certified as Air Worthy to pass inspection. This plane had a LOW wing, manufactured in plywood! The fuselage itself was fabric. I spent hour after hour on my back sanding that plywood, to no avail!

Also about that time I was billed several hundred dollars by the State for taxes, and I had no alternative but to sell my plane. I sold it to another airport for just $50, where the engine was then mounted on a stand in an Orange Orchard, to circulate air during cold temperatures.

Oh well, at least I can say *I once owned my own Airplane!*

An Unhappy Ending

Eventually a gasoline shortage occurred, which made local airplane flights impractical.
Brackett Field was shut down for many months, and with it, the dream Jack and I had to become Missionaries for Jungle Aviation came to an end.

About six months later I decided to make a visit for old time sake. I walked up to the office, in a happy mood and asked, *"Where's Steve?"* I had nothing but quiet stares.
Eventually one of the staffers asked, *"You don't know?"* I said, *"Know what?"*

"Steve drove his car to the end of the runway...

*then ran a hose from his tailpipe INTO the car, and he **committed suicide**!"*

That explained how deeply Steve's quietness and PTSD had remained with him for all those years of flying cargo over the hump between Burma, India and China

Visulite Illustrated Sermons

Location: Azusa, California. Status, Junior year at Pacific Bible College.

There was a time of personal questioning about my future ministry, when I recalled a time when a Chalk Artist made his message visually, rather than just standing up behind a pulpit. Part of what impressed me most, was that he used a brilliant colored chalk. I learned later than he also used what is known as Ultra Violet light aimed at his visuals. I still recall that his message showed people approaching an open, burning pit, with people jumping into Hell. He pointed out scriptures telling the way as being "Broad, and many there be who enter therein!'"

So I set out to develop a sermon that would be so different that people would both see, hear, and be drawn to a different type of preaching. So I did the following:
(1) Find out about Ultra Violet light.
(2) Design a portable stage.
(3) Add colored light to that stage
(4) Use music and sound effects. (A tape recorder would make that possible.)
(5) Use a movie projector for action.

I am second from the left in our Quartet

Obviously I would need other people to assist. The photo of 4 young men would fulfill that job. (I'm second from left side. Note we all wore white dress jackets.)

In the photo we stood in front of a white movie screen. Moviegoers in that day and age heard audio thru the screen, because there were thousands of small holes in it. Sound blasted through what appeared to be solid. In theaters today, Surround Sound speakers hang on walls near the audience.

Our program began with a Trumpet Trio, played by the three boys. They were so talented, that in one Pasadena Rose Parade they were the lead-off performers. Next, I joined them to form a male quartet, and later I sang a solo. Going back to the movie screen, several colored lights were directed on it, unless I wanted them turned down. In those instances, we made that "solid screen" disappear. At that point we brought up lights pointed about 3' behind the screen, aimed backwards.

Another screen (operated by two of the boys) re-created the Biblical scene where King Belshazzar saw handwriting on a wall. He was told he was weighed in the balances and found wanting. We illustrated that movement. In another scene we used a "scrim" effect, which made a hollow facial feature of Jesus appear. The effect was to cause our audience to think of their personal relationship with Him!

I also operated a movie projector standing alone in the midst of our audience. Wires ran to the stage, and were connected to a small 2"x3" box hooked to my belt. With that box I controlled a tape recorder, the power on and off and volume.

Prior to our performance I powdered my face and hands with Ultra-Violet powder. At a critical scene, I was able to turn the projector on suddenly, with the explosion of an Atomic Bomb. Then I also opened the shutter of a UV light, and froze still. I looked totally green! Kids in the front row went screaming back to their family.

At the end of the first evening there was no doubt the VisuLite sermon was very effective. It was done at a church near Pacific Bible College. The next thing was to line up performances elsewhere. It was summer, and I lined up the message upstate in California, to Central California, and on up north into Oregon.

This is where God apparently wanted me to learn some lessons about His future plans for me. At each location, We were at the mercy of several factors: attendance was determined by:
(a) How well the Pastor of each church publicized the event
(b) Size of the town
(c) Weather conditions,
(d) Other events scheduled in the town, etc. and whether or not offerings covered our expenses!
Results? Not encouraging!

Enter "Sermons From Science!"

Moody Institute of Science in Santa Monica,

California produced amazing color films which dealt with scientific studies of nature. One of the physicists saw my Visu-lite Illustrated Sermon, and invited me to join that organization. Keith Hargett directed a road show which gave live performances in various cities, Fairs, and Military bases across the U.S. His Sermons From Science two hour exhibitions were amazing, and well known nationwide. Dr. Irwin Moon was the Director of all Sermons From Science activities.

For the assignment I went on with Mr. Hargett, he purchased a new Air Stream travel trailer. The trailer was just a shell, with interior floor space for $40,000 worth of portable scientific equipment.

The messages of all public performances dealt with the limits human beings have with regard to sight, sound, and existence. Example: Demonstrations pointed out that we are 99.9% blind to vistas of sight... X-rays, Delta rays, Beta rays, Cosmic rays, Ultra Violet rays and many others. He stated we only see 1 tenth of 1% of light all around us.

In the area of sound, we also are deaf to many sources surrounding us. He went into detail about the Speed of Light, Distances to other heavenly bodies, etc. Being in tune and out of tune to the many forces around us are pretty well known today. But in the times when Sermons From Science was active, the public was uneducated and fascinated by education and demonstrations!

A Million Volts Of Electricity

By far the most famous of the "Moody Sermons From Science" demonstrations was watching Dr. Irwin Moon, or either of his two traveling Physicists, stand on a coil of wire, and take a Million volts of Electricity through their bodies! The illustration was intended to show how it is possible to be IN tune or OUT of tune spiritually to Gods plan for our lives!

Physicist Keith Hargett and I put on our first performance in San Diego California in an auditorium seating about 2,000 people. In the early part of his lecture, Hargett was to speak in detail about many of the concepts I referred to earlier. However, that demonstration of taking high voltage through his body almost turned out to be disastrous!

On that Sunday, during the process of unloading all the equipment from our trailer, Keith found out that the 3' tall by 18" wide coil of wire had been damaged. Repairing that coil meant we had to purchase new wire and re-wrap it. Problem: Electric Repair shops were closed on Sundays, and the only wire we found was smaller. We spent much of the day replacing the coil, but there was no time to test the coil, nor how well Keith's body would react to smaller wire!

Performance time: Keith had run heavy duty wire from the auditoriums 220 volt switching room and transferred it to us on stage. Several 6' cabinets housed our equipment. One of those cabinets, called an Oden Resonator, generated high voltage, which made a whirring sound. I controlled the on-off switch, which looked like a pistol. When I squeezed that pistol, all the house lights would go off instantly, and lightning would thunder out of Keith's hands held above his body! I was nervous! Was I about to send a man to his death? Keith was nervous also, because he knew how painful this un-tested event might be!

He had to use a stool to step atop the 3' high coil of wire. Once there, he had to be careful, or die in the process. It was necessary to extend his arms as far above his head as possible or it would cook his brains. At his fingertips he held thimbles with 1" long spikes, from which the million volts of lightning would radiate!

Keith wore a dark blue coat and white shirt. *Thank God for that White shirt!*
Here goes... He called out to me to fire the pistol switch, *"Ready... **Hit it!"*** Keith screamed, and started to fall! In the darkness all I could see was his white shirt falling and I

cut the power! He landed on his feet, but was sick! There were burn marks on his hands where the voltage had escaped! You could almost hear a pin drop in the auditorium! Keith somehow managed to end the performance.

That was the last time Keith attempted to take that lightning through his body. However, he did place a silver bowl with firecrackers on top of the coil. Future performances went off with a *BANG* and blue bolts of lightning!

"Fireworks"

A number of the Sermons From Science demonstrations were performed at US Air Force bases, under the Chaplains' Character Guidance program.

Many of the cadets did not look forward to another boring lecture.

Keith Hargett had a way of changing their minds about the boring part, quickly!

You may recall I mentioned he no longer stood on a coil of wire, which shot 1,000,000 volts of lightning upwards. Now he placed an 18" cup shaped silver bowl atop the 3' tall coil of wire. We placed firecrackers on top, so when Keith hit high voltage, their was a loud *"BANG"* followed by about 10' of lightning!

When the show was about to begin, Keith never said a word. He simply turned on the Oden Resonator, hit the switch, followed by fireworks and lightning! Men in the front row thought they'd been shot. Then Keith reached under his desk and tossed out a roll of toilet paper. He asked, "Does any body in the front row need this?" Howls of laughter followed, and from that point on, they were ready to listen to whatever Keith said.

We were at an Air Force base about 30 miles from Houston Texas on one occasion. We were low on firecrackers, and because there were fireworks plants in Houston, Keith sent me into town to stock up on the noisemakers while he prepared for an afternoon performance at 3pm.

In town I visited both of the two Fireworks plants, and at one plant I bought a large box. I still remember that very large case cost $64. Then as a sales lady began to wheel that case out for me, I looked up. There were hundreds of cases stacked about 50' high. I was impressed at the quantity, and asked what unknowingly turned out be a prophetic question. I said *"Lady if these firecrackers ever exploded they'd go sky high, wouldn't they?"* She just chuckled and replied, *"Oh, they're all pretty much fire proofed!"*
With my case on board, I drove back to the base 30 miles away, in time to help with the performance.

The next morning at breakfast, Keith and I were eating. Over his shoulder I saw a newspaper stand, and noticed the headlines. Keith asked me, *"What's wrong? You look white as a sheet!"* The newspaper headlines read *"3 people killed, 9 injured in Fireworks Plant explosion!"* **It happened 20 minutes after 1 left**

that plant! Thank you God for protecting me!
Leaving SFS

I spent about 9 months on the road with Sermons From Science, but left in time to finish my last term and graduate from Pacific Bible College. Those months on the road were priceless!

Sermons From Science as an organization also recognized that television was making changes to society. Just as I had experienced, being able to minister in a single location was more practical, economical, and reached more people than traveling! Eventually Moody Institute of Science made changes to their own ministry, and it's location in California.

Thank God for "Sermons From Science!"

TV Career

About the time I graduated from Pacific Bible College with a degree in Bible Theology, I took a part-time job in a store where television sets were being sold by the dozens. My job was to prepare cabinets and TV sets for sale and delivery. The owners of the store were selling so many sets that it became very evident to me that we were now living in a new age, and that radio's heyday had passed! Now, television was the predominant field of interest.

This was God's way of encouraging me to pursue a Master's Degree in Television Production in Los Angeles, California. After completion of training, and graduation, I was accepted as a Production Director for a large TV Station in Stockton, California.

The station had a large staff and good-sized Production stage. On Saturday evenings we had a 2 hour live show with about 4 camera operators, and well experienced Switcher/Director operators. I was thrilled to be able to fill in wherever it was necessary to make the show run smoothly. I loved it!

Then the balloon burst! The entire station was bought out by another firm in San Francisco. The frequency (channel) was part of the purchase, and 13 of us on the staff were given our final paychecks and were removed from the staff! Ouch, that hurt!

Did God still have TV as a part of my career? Naturally! He was still at the helm of my life, and He continued to be the Compass, directing every course He planned to send me.

Sending out my resume, it wasn't too long before I had a phone call from a Bill Smullin, owner of radio and TV stations operating out of Eureka, California. Mr. Smullin offered to pay my expenses for a meeting with him, whether or not he hired me. He was a very special man who was honorable in every aspect of his life.

KIEM-TV Eureka was a small station with a very small staff. Everyone did a multitude of tasks, in a very few minutes of station operations. Talk about learning. Again, God had His good reasons! It wasn't too long before Bill Smullin did another great thing for me, he sent me to a six week training school in Los Angeles, to learn how to pass an FCC 1st class Engineers License. The tests and examinations took us about 14 hours a day.

That Engineer's License opened doors for Television and Radio station operations beyond any mere basic studio duties.

Transmitter Sites

With my Engineer's license in hand, now I was given assignments to run mountain top Transmitter sites. In Eureka, KIEM-TV's signal was transmitted from a high mountaintop from a 5-kilowatt transmitter. Transmitters were typically about 10' long, by 4' thick and 8' tall. The units were very noisy and required circulation of a lot of air, to cool the units.

My first experience on the Eureka transmitter site required a drive to a mountaintop about 18 miles from the studio. I still remember having to walk about 200 yards uphill through snow several feet deep. I had never worn snowshoes before, and it was a new experience.

Then in the spring one evening after shutting down the signal, I climbed aboard the company pickup truck for the return to town. After driving only a short distance, I was approaching a right hand turn which was the start of a straight nine mile downhill grade. I put on the brake to slow down, but "clunk," the brake pedal went flat to the floorboards. That required an immediate decision! God gave me the wisdom just to quickly turn the truck into the left side uphill embankment, which stopped the truck just in time. The only thing left to do was curl up on the seat and pray that someone from the studio would come looking for me. About 2 am, a staffer did come looking for me. Boy was he welcome. Apparently a hose in the brake system had come loose.

In those days satellite systems were unheard of. In order to relay signals over great distances, it was necessary to install an unmanned microwave site in a remote region. Two men were sent in to one of those locations, which proved to be fatal for them. A large snowstorm caused the men to be lost. Search parties spent about two months seeking to find the men, and it was spring time before their bodies were found. Apparently the two crawled under an out cropped rock for shelter and froze to death. Dozens of searchers had walked within a few feet of the men, but bushes had hid them. Bill Smullin paid the two widows the monthly salaries of each man, for as long as the widows lived.

One summer I was sent from Eureka, California to Medford, Oregon to cover the summer vacations of transmitter engineers. Summer heat was at its peak. Temperatures of over 100 were normal. Along about sundown, I felt it might be now cool enough outside, that I could step outside and get away from the noise and heat of the transmitter. Then all of a sudden I felt like a 16 year old kid, and rather than stepping outside, I LEAPED outside. In middle of the jump, I looked down, and saw a rattlesnake. If I had stepped outside, that snake would have nailed me!

God was definitely the One who caused me to be a kid again. *Thank you. Lord!*

Television In Klamath Falls!

In the area Bill Smullin sought to add to his Broadcast Stations, Klamath Falls was a strategic location. He already had a TV Station in Medford Oregon, plus another in Redding California. Please understand that Television was in its infancy.

That's where a high peak called Plum Ridge was ideal. It was actually a mile high, and overlooked the community called the Klamath Basin. KOTI-TV was appropriately named and advertised as Oregon's Mile High station! That peak is where a tall antenna, and building to house the transmitter were located. It also had another advantage, in that we could pick up the Medford station, and feed their programs directly into our transmitter!

One more great advantage was that our studio could be located only a few hundred feet downhill, on the campus of a WWII military base. That base was built for members of the Service who had acquired Malaria in the jungles where they fought.

As it was being phased out, a man by the name of Dr. Winston Purvine acquired the entire campus for only $1. He organized a hands-on training school, which he named

"Oregon Technical Institute"
Do you notice the letters O-T-I in the TV stations'
call letters?
While today, that training school is a full University, in the very beginning it trained future workers in almost any trade you can think of: Auto or Diesel Mechanic, Electrician, how to type, Structural Engineering, Animal Husbandry, and a host of practical skills needed in many fields of Labor.

Note: Skills, rather than text book instruction in a class room, is what has allowed graduates of Oregon Institute of Technology to find employment easier and more quickly than many other universities.

The actual campus of OTI was in a small canyon. Administration Offices, a track, covered gymnasium, and a host of other shops and classrooms for learning. There were Dorms made up of double-story living quarters also.

The KOTI -TV STUDIO

One of the two story Dormitories became our studio and offices. Adjacent to them, we cut out the entire upper floor of the main building, which allowed us to hang the many lights a television studio requires. Also, we used black pitch slapped on the walls, to which rolls of insulation were added. They were to deaden echoes, and to allow a sense of quiet within the studio.

Me operating the studio camera at KOTI.

The dimensions I have from memory is that the studio was about 40' X 40' square, plus about 25' high. The military built floor was terrible! Long strips of wood were only about 4 INCHES wide, which meant that when we had to dolly (move) our camera, it made the picture bounce like ocean waves! (There was no such thing as a zoom lens for our one and only camera.) The camera had 3 front lenses for shooting objects different lengths away. Also, we didn't change the lenses on air. Therefore, we had to do a lot of advance planning to determine where our tv cameras were placed, especially when we needed to view certain objects, such as an automobile, followed by a price tag.

Captain Uncle Bill Show

The Russians had just launched the first Sputnik into space, and the world was fascinated with Rocket ships. So, I had an idea, *why not start a kid's Rocket Ship show?* It was a hit right away! In one corner of our studio, we drew on large cardboard a drawing which looked like a window of a rocket ship! Someone built a 6' tall Robot, whom I named *"Robby the robot!"*

Problem: How do I make him talk? Solution: Record my own voice ahead of time, on a tape recorder. Then when Robby was supposed to talk to me, the camera operator would zero in on him. At that time I reached down to the recorder, out of sight at my feet, and played my own voice back at half speed! So when I asked Robby, "Whose our Sponsor?" He would slowly say, *"Meh doe Bell!"* (Medobell Milk) No mouth movement! No matter, the kids and my sponsor were happy!

There usually were about a dozen kids, sitting on a two step bench. Sometimes there were young Boy or Girl Scout Troops. Other times one of the kids might have a Birthday, and Mom would bring a Birthday cake, which we all shared, and sang Happy Birthday

Each student received an Official Membership Card, verifying that he or she was a member of "Captain Uncle Bill's Outer Space Club!" Including pre-flight training, and having completed a flight aboard the rocket ship X-TV2!

Robby the Robot!

I had periodic contests where viewers would compete for a Rocket Ship of their own. They were to send me drawings of a Rocket ship (most of them used a Medobell Milk carton blasting off). The winner would appear on the show, and I gave them a cardboard Rocket ship, which was large enough for them to climb inside, and close the hatch over them.

After 20 minutes of interviews, or games, it was time for us to shout aloud: "**5...4...3...2...1... Blast off!**" to Cartoon Land!

Newscaster

Being a Newscaster has it's positive and negative features:

(1) Many people place both local, State and National News as a high priority for viewing time. Hence the Newsman has a large viewing audience.

(2) The News person knows more about events present and future than most other people in the vicinity.

When I became KOTI-TV's News Director, I met many famous people...especially politicians. Not only local well knowns, but Governors and even Presidential candidates. Richard Nixon was running for US President at a Rally in Tulelake. I recall he played a piano and made witty comments to the audience. I took his picture with my Polaroid camera, and gave it to him backstage. Governor Hatfield was a Christian, who later became a US Senator. He had a great memory, and always called me Bill as a friend and brother.

Doing the News at KOTI.

People seemed to go out of their way to make my acquaintance. The Air Force at Kingsley Field gave me a ride in a T-33 Training Jet, as VIP of the Month. It was a thrill to go thru the process of being fitted into a cockpit and being shown what procedures to follow in an emergency. Then it was *"Take Off"* for a ride to Crater Lake and back, including the opportunity to take over the controls, and fly the jet on my own.

My VIP flight in a T-33.

While the positive side of being a News Director was great...there was also a very painful side! It left me with gruesome memories I shall never forget as long as I live!

One of my first on-the-scene events took me about 3 miles south of Henley schools, to a double railroad crossing. A train had hit a car, and I keenly recall seeing an arm and a leg lying beside the train track. I still recall many car wrecks. One of them a suicide by intentionally running directly into the path of a truck. I saw a jet plane that had crashed into a back yard in the Stewart Lennox area. A murder in the Ross Ragland Theater while a movie was being shown. I still see in my memories drops of blood dripping from a

Coroner's table. Are you still with me? How about Fires? The Fire Department loaned me a pair of Firemen's boots to place by my bed. When an evening fire call came, I only had to jump into those boots and take off for the fire.

On one such fire, a house burned near a Lumberyard, and was basically contained that night. But the next morning I returned for further information. Walking around the house,
I looked into a children's bedroom, and thought I was looking at charred baby dolls, only to realize to my horror, that those were not dolls... *but the Kids!* (I can still remember the emotions I felt for about a week.) Neither I nor the Firemen had any appetite for food that week.

One more story

There was a dam not far from a bridge near the Klamath Falls Moore Park. Two young boys had walked to the dam to go fishing. One of the boys slipped and fell, hitting his head on the concrete, and drowned. I was called to the scene, taking a 16mm movie camera along to take photos of the scene for news coverage. Firemen were trying to revive the boy. I bent over with the camera and was trying to get a close-up. But a voice in my head cried **"No!"** *This is a sacred moment. You don't belong here!* I had no choice...this was my Job!

Then an even more painful, living voice: It was the boy's grandmother. To her, I was a member of her family, because I was on TV every night in the family living room! She cried out, looking to me for help! **"Bill, what am I gonna do? He watched your show every night!"**

Again, this was my job... I had no choice but to leave her all alone, with no answers.
Over the years this story more than any others, haunts me!

Yes, I'm in tears as I write!

Electronic Demons

To the Reader:

I have two reasons for highlighting the division "Electronic Demons"

1. It amplifies that the book is now showing a Division: the old past stories with a new phase and time.
2. I use the metaphor of "demons" in all the El Cajon stories. (I also encountered the similar type of conflicts in another station I put on the air in Merced, CA later on.)

3. Most Christians complain about the trash we see and hear on TV. I fully believe in the "Electronic Demons." I hope our readers may pick up on the reality of how Satan works in the media.

Electronic Demons!

The purpose of this story is not to establish the existence of Electronic Demons, but is something I've often wondered about, after experiencing many weird events in Christian radio.

Most of my life has been centered around the operation and management of radio and TV stations, both commercial and listener supported.

My skills are in announcing and production, rather than in the engineering side. Each of those skills involves different types of personalities. Although I did pass an FCC First Class Engineers examination, the technical expertise is not my in-born gift.

Unfortunately, the need for technical background happened when I was all alone, in a strange new city, and about to enter a phase of broadcasting unfamiliar to me, non-commercial FM Radio.

I had worked for the previous seven years in Oregon, as a Television Announcer. In addition to having produced hundreds of commercials, I also had the daily 6 O' Clock News and a much watched Captain Uncle Bill kids show. In commercial TV, our cameras and equipment performed well.

But now, in non-Commercial Christian radio, I was about to encounter forces diabolically opposed to spreading the Gospel over the air Waves. The Bible verse Ephesians 2:2 refers to Satan as the "Prince of the power of the air." Interestingly, broadcasters use the term power in referring to the number of watts or kilowatts a station is approved to transmit.

Putting a new FM station on the air!

Before launching out into the battle of airwaves, let me explain who my employers were: They were Family Radio Network in San Francisco, California. The flagship for this network was KEAR-FM in the bay area. KEBR-FM was their Sacramento station, and KECR-FM El Cajon, was the station I was assigned to cover San Diego. This new station was originally operated by other owners, but had not been able to make it pay off.

During the silent years of the old station, a TV Cable Company had put up a Television Booster station of low power, in our vicinity. It was used to relay weak TV signals in Los Angeles, 80 miles away, and retransmit TV to El Cajon. Uh Oh! Our FM Station was only 30' away, and was about to saturate the TV signals.

Studio/Transmitter

Normally, studios and transmitter buildings are separate. But in the case of KECR-FM, both were located in the same small building, and noise from the transmitter fans could be heard when a microphone was turned on.

An engineer from Family Radio headquarters explained quickly to me how to tune the transmitter. Peak one meter, on another meter look for a minimum reading, etc, etc. That equipment was new to me, and I really didn't understand, nor remember a lot of his instructions. Having said all that, he bid me good-bye, and headed off to San Francisco.

Going On The Air!
Was I ever excited? I could hardly wait. Let's do it! Flip the main turn table on...fill the air with awesome, inspirational music.! It was beautiful... now fade the music down & under, as I opened the microphone. *"Helloooo San Diego! This is KECR FM El Cajon, your brand NEW Christian station! If you hear us, please give me a phone call, and let us know how you like the music!"*

It wasn't too long before our first call came in. A lady said, *"Yes, the music does sound nice, but shouldn't it be on just ONE spot on the dial, rather than all over it?"* Uh Oh.... I began to sweat! The next call wasn't so cordial. An angry man shouted to me, *"What are you doing in the middle of Channel 8 on Television?"* By this time I knew KECR had a **big** problem! Now what do I do?

The FCC steps in!
Next morning a car drove into the parking lot, and a polite gentleman showed me his credentials and badge. In the backseat of his car were several large radio receivers, capable of measuring precise frequencies! The nice man said, *"Come on Son, Let's go for a ride and listen to your signal."*

Now I did want our station to be heard, but not in places it was <u>not supposed</u> to be heard! The further he drove away from our transmitter, the weaker our main signal became, while the unwanted harmonic signal got stronger. I slid down in the car seat and wanted to disappear, or wake up, and I'd find it was only a bad dream!

By way of explanation: A harmonic signal is either half of the allotted frequency, or double it. In this case, the sub harmonic signal was stronger than where we were supposed to be! Problem: How do we reduce the unwanted signal, and increase the proper frequency?

Problem Solving

I made frantic phone calls to local FM broadcast stations, and asked engineers for their advice about what to do. The answers were, *"Call a guy named Charlie Sharbino. He's a harmonic expert. If anybody can help you, Charlie can!"* Charlie's price was out of sight, but there was no other option. So it wasn't long before Charlie came out to our transmitter site. His best suggestion was to wrap the entire small building in chicken wire, then solder the wire in lots of places, and attach them to rods pounded into the ground. That didn't work at all. Were Electronic Demons grinning? Maybe, but God had future reasons for our meeting him!

Meanwhile the Cable TV company was having fits. Their warning was *"Clean up the signals from that blankety blank FM station, or get it off the Air! We'll sue you!"*

I pleaded with Family Radio to send that Engineer back to San Diego! At long last he did arrive, and in about 30 minutes he had rewired what is called The Exciter circuit, and eliminated the unwanted harmonic to within legal limits. Legal limits meant within a few hundred yards of the site.

However, that TV booster amplifier was still only 30' away from our 3,000 watts. I drove to the Cable office and met with the Manager. I apologized for the problems, but announced to him that we were now within legal limits. He replied, *"Is that so? We'll just see about that!"* and he reached for his phone to call an attorney! On his desk was a TV Monitor, which showed lines of interference across his set. Meantime I'm in a panic, and prayed up a storm. *"Lord please! You've just got to DO something about this. I don't know what to do! Please Lord Help!"*

He DID hear, and gave me miracle! All of a sudden it looked like a giant hand started at one side of the TV screen and moved slowly across the picture, leaving it clear as a bell!

As the manager put his phone down, I asked to use it, and called the volunteer transmitter operator. I asked *"What did you do to the transmitter?"* He said, *"Nothing at all. I'm just sitting here!"*

Our interference problems were gone for good!

If Demons were keeping score... let it show they are now down by 2 points!
Thanks Lord!

Getting Volunteers

It was impossible for me to operate the station alone, so in response to over-the-air requests for volunteer operators, people began to show up to keep the station on the air. All announcements were prerecorded on tape, so announcing was not required. All went smoothly until one high school student innocently sent a notice of Work Study to a government office. Next thing I knew, a representative of HEW (Health Education and Welfare) called, and accused me of trying to get free labor out of juveniles. 1 told him we were a non-profit Christian organization, sold no advertising at all, and that the operators volunteered on their own to help us in ministry.

The HEW dude didn't buy it! Even after 1 mailed him a copy of the Family Radio Charter, listing us as a Tax Deductible ministry, he still insisted we pay each volunteer two months of back wages. With what? Listener support did not yet cover our expenses, and this man was going to take us to Court! I was desperate, discouraged, and at my wit's end!

On The Carpet!

Literally, that's what I did. Flat on my face on a living room carpet, I asked *"Why Lord? Isn't this opposition ever going to end?"* Now I've heard of people having visions, but I never quite knew how to accept them. I did NOT ask for one, **but God's answer was just that!** For the first and only time in life, *I had a vision!*

I didn't see anything with my eyes, but very clearly in my mind! Eyes closed in prayer, I saw the upper right hand corner page of a Bible, with the words of Ephesians 6: 12 *"For we wrestle not against flesh and blood, but against Principalities and Powers...against spiritual forces in high places!"* A shaft of light beamed down flashing on and off on the words, *Principalities and Powers... Principalities and Powers!*

I sat bolt upright with new understanding! In my past life, the spiritual struggles I'd had were between just two people, Satan and me...one on one. But now my efforts involved the spiritual fate of thousands of people in San Diego who needed to hear how Jesus could change their lives. So, as the Prince of the Power of the air Satan wasn't about to take KECR-FM lying down! That's where the radio harmonics and interference came from. That's also why the HEW man was trying to make our ministries impossible!

WOW!   What a revelation that was!   Praise
The Lord!

Pilgrims Progress

The trouble was, we still had a problem. What could be done about the HEW man who wanted us to pay volunteers two months back wages, when we had no income yet? Solution? *More Time on the Carpet!*

Then the Lord reminded me of John Bunyan's famous story *"Pilgrim's Progress."*
It's the story about a man called Christian, also named Pilgrim. Pilgrim was making his way through life toward a place called the Celestial City (Heaven.) As he struggles through life, Christian would face deep periods of challenge and depression. The Slough of Despondency, or enticements into sin at Vanity Fair's pleasures were fearful. At other times Christian was led astray by people who made him doubt, or attempted to divert him from his journey toward the Celestial City.

In one fearful scene, Pilgrim saw Lions in the path ahead. The Lion's roar scared Pilgrim so badly that he almost turned and ran. But the call of the Celestial City would not let up. He just had to go forward! Getting more afraid with each step, he took a closer look at the Lions. When Pilgrim came over a slight rise in the path ahead, he did indeed see Lions on either side of the path. But upon closer look, each of the Lions had a band around his neck that was attached to a chain, that only let him reach the edge of the path, and no further! Therefore, as long as Christian stayed in the middle of the path, there was no way the Lions could hurt him!

Remembering that story was my cue; *March forward and let God take care of HEW!*
I called HEW and told the man that we stood by our statement that we had no desire to take advantage of free labor from our volunteers. If he cared to press legal charges that was up to him! We had no fear of any wrongdoing. Result? The man did come out to meet with our Volunteers, all of whom assured him they were performing their duties for the Lord, to keep Christian radio on the air!

Demons lose again!

Signal Boxed In!

The name *El Cajon* is the Spanish word for box or canyon. And that is exactly what this suburb of San Diego was...a growing community nestled in a canyon outside of San Diego proper.

To better understand the land: Beginning right moving left, <u>think</u> San Diego city on the right Mt. Helix is almost center, then moving left again is El Cajon suburb! Now moving left again and UP is a tall, long mountain range overlooking the entire area!

The KECR-FM transmitter overlooked El Cajon, but was below Mt. Helix! It is important to know that Mt. Helix had multi-million dollar mansions over the entire cone, and blocked our signal to San Diego proper. More than once I thought of the Bible verse that says, *"If we have faith, we can move mountains!"* So moving Mt. Helix became my great desire!

Earlier, 1 mentioned Charlie Sharbino, the harmonic expert I hired to solve our interference problems. He had mentioned owning property at *La Cresta*, the small community on the mountain range east that was overlooking El Cajon. I became fascinated with that hilltop. Day after day I'd gaze up at the location and dream of moving KECR-FM's transmitter to that area. High mountains were not hard to find, but finding one with electric power was a problem.

One day, binoculars to my eyes, I noticed a line of power poles going up toward La Cresta, but the last pole stopped halfway up the hill. I wondered why it stopped. Curious to know why, I decided to drive up a canyon road, and arrived at La Cresta from the rear. The road closest to El Cajon was a dead end dirt road, blocked by a locked gate. Parking the car, I climbed over the gate and walked about 400 yards uphill, hoping to find that power pole.

Miracle Spot!

Approaching a power pole up ahead I could see it did have electric power. This must be the pole I'd seen from down in the valley! Then I walked up to the pole, and gazed in amazement, at a panorama that was breathtaking! At my feet was all of El Cajon! Then lifting my gaze I could easily see *over Mt. Helix, and in the distance:* **San Diego itself!**

It was an incredible view, and I whispered, *"Praise God! Lord, can we move here?"* Then as if in a direct answer, my gaze shifted to the right, and wonder of wonders... I saw something I'll never forget as long as I live: **There about 30' to my right was a 12' by 24' concrete slab and foundation already poured and ready for a building to be placed on it!** I was stunned! God had led me to this secluded spot in His own Mysterious Ways and timing!

How did that foundation and slab get there? Upon investigation, I learned that a Fraternal Organization had, in years past, used this spot to conduct their secret initiation rites. (Possibly in a Quonset hut.) It was all part of God's Plan. He knew years earlier that someday this spot would be an ideal location for *HIS* radio station to spread the Gospel to thousands of people! Praise The Lord!

Family Radio arranged a five year lease of the property. Within months we had received approval from the FCC to move KECR-FM to this location. We built a new building. Most importantly, we were able to increase our transmitter power from only 3,000 watts to 15,000 watts, at a 1500' higher elevation. In FM radio, high elevations are critical for good signal coverage. This meant that for the first time, many San Diegans could hear *life changing* Christian music and messages!

KECR Grows!

It wasn't long before we acquired a downtown El Cajon studio, and were able to hire part time employees. Everything looked much rosier. Interference was gone, coverage was improved and lives were being changed by the Lord.

But Satan and his demons were not through with us yet!

Fire in the mountains!

The mountain range where our transmitter was located, ran in a long northerly direction and consisted of mostly of brush and small trees. Then one hot summer day a fire started way up north, and began to burn out of control in our direction. The strong wind driven flames soared high in the sky, and skipped from one peak to another at racecar speed. Nothing stopped the flames. Down in the valley we watched helplessly as the fire roared closer to La Cresta and the KECR transmitter building. Was this another horde of demons sent to destroy us for good?

We prayed earnestly... *"Please God, save our transmitter!"* Then another miracle! Only a hundred yards from our station, the winds suddenly shifted, and the flames shot off in another direction!

Saved again by our protective, ever-vigilant Lord!
Another Mountain!

Even with the improved signal from La Cresta, the KECR coverage of San Diego was spotty. Many times I gazed in a southerly direction at another mountain named Mt. Miguel. It towered high above the city, and could be seen for miles. The problem was, there was no road to the top, and no electric power. I prayed, *"Lord, what about Mt. Miguel?"*

Yes, God knew it was an even better mountain. So did other broadcasters, who got together and built a road, plus power lines to the top of Mt. Miguel. Then most of the San Diego stations moved their transmitters atop Miguel, *including KECR!* Signal coverage from that spot is incredible! Even listeners across the border into Mexico could now hear the lifesaving message of Jesus. Our message was, *"For a change in your life, listen to Family Radio!"*

Unfortunately, I was not there to see the move. I had new assignments to other Christian stations in Virginia, California, and Oregon. At one new Christian FM station I again encountered electronic opposition, which I attributed to the Prince of the Power of the air! He may indeed have electronic demons working for him. I for one suspect it to be

TRUE!

However, another Bible verse states, *"Greater is He who is in you, than he who is in the World!"*

Count On It!

"Caesar's Discovery"

Years ago I became interested in using a 16mm movie camera while I was employed at a television station. Shortly after that, 1 felt called to ministry. Still in Broadcasting, I moved to the San Diego California area to manage a Christian radio station. I had produced short 1 minute TV commercials in a studio where we had normal equipment to add a sound track, slides, and whatever else was needed.

Somehow word got out to missionaries about my camera, and they asked if I would be willing to make a movie about their ministry with Mexican youth. They had a ministry in a church to Mexican families on the U.S. side of the border. What they really wanted promoted was their summer ministry for young people in a summer camp. That campground was several hundred miles into a forested area in the Baja's! (pronounced Ba ha's).

I would have to shoot the film with NO audio, and add the sound track later. To begin the movie, I drove to a Mexican church located on the US side of the border. Here I met a teenage boy, and took scenes of him shooting baskets on a basketball court. His real name was not Caesar, but that was the name I chose for the movie.

Shortly after that, he and the missionaries drove by car to the summer camp. Their drive was over a narrow, bumpy path thru the mountains barely wide enough for a single car. If their car broke down, they could be stranded for hours, almost helpless. I mention this because that is what really happened on their return trip home, and I was with them. More about this later.

Air Plane Ride

Because my duties at the new radio station kept me busy, the Missionaries decided to rent an airplane and fly me to the Youth Summer camp. The plane was a low wing, single propeller plane. I still remember that there was no airport, simply a dry lake bed to land on. When the engine was shut down, the propeller simply stopped. Many months later, that simple visual scene which I had taken with my movie camera, had to be given an audio sound track. My radio station Engineer, Dennis Sherbino, came up with an ingenious idea of listening to disc recordings of many sound tracks. The only airplane sound he came up with was a jet plane taking off. He simply recorded that jet sound, then reversed the sound and slowed it down to a stop. That duplicated the propeller being stopped.

Summer Camp

Caesar and the other teenagers were already at the campground. It is very important for you to know that Caesar did not speak English, and I knew no Spanish. So the two of us began to teach each other how to learn a new language. Two of the first words he taught me were life saving! As the two of us walked up a hill towards the dining room, he pointed to the path we were walking on and said, *"Cuidado, Beebelo!"* **"Be careful, rattle snake!"** That caught my attention fast.

Then, in the chow hall during lunch, I pointed toward a jar of cheese sprinkles, and asked him in English to, "Please pass the Cheese." He cracked up in laughter, because I had asked him to "Pass Gas!" For the rest of summer camp I took movie scenes of him and other campers enjoying the normal outdoor life, Bible studies and learning experiences typical of any Christian camp.

Remember earlier I mentioned the narrow, bumpy road through the mountains to get to camp? I said if a car broke down the occupants could be stranded for hours? The reason I came back via this road rather than by plane, was so I could get footage on film!

When the Missionaries' car stopped running, we all did a lot of praying! Eventually a Mexican man on his way home in the mountains stopped and looked under the hood of our vehicle. He then went home, and came back with the very fuel pump we needed! PRAISE THE LORD!

JoseLNU

It has been many decades past since I have had contact with Caesar.

Moments ago we made contact again, and he gave me an ok to use a portion of his present name for safety reasons. LNU means, "last name unidentified." Later in this story you'll be able to understand the reason why. Jose is a common first name of Mexican males. So let me pickup where we left off, the return trip from Summer Youth camp.

Jose returned to his home in Tijuana, Mexico, south of San Diego, California. It wasn't very long before details of Jose's birth were known. His mother waded across the Rio Grande river when she was in labor for her son to be born. A mid-wife delivered the boy, and signed off the details: Mother's name and pertinent details, the boy's name, date, location of birth, etc.

I knew a secretary in San Diego who worked in an Attorney's Office. She took that information and was able to then issue a Birth Certificate of US Citizenship! Jose xxxx!

Since he didn't have any place to live, I decided to let him live with me for a while. I found his home in Tijuana's City Dump. Nine family members had taken shelter under a 5' high metal shack, roughly 12' across. Though it was broad daylight outside, I could barely see the interior (not that the awful odor gave me any desire to search).

Driving away, I had to roll my windows down to get a breath of fresh air. We relived that day recently, and Jose said he knew why I had rolled the windows down, but he couldn't do anything about it.

I had an idea: *Why not treat Jose to his first Hamburger?* As we approached the entrance, he wanted to be polite and open the door for me. However, the Jack In The Box door opened automatically, and Jose jumped back in astonishment!

Jose Moves In

Now that Jose was a US citizen, he had some real adjustments to make in **who** he now was and how to move forward.

Dennis Sherbino-Engineer, Jose Ortez and me.

I had no extra bedroom for him, so he volunteered to just curl up on a corner of my living room on the carpet. He loved it, as we probably would feel on a new feather bed.

There were some mornings when I found some items missing from my refrigerator, but so what? I certainly could not blame him in the least. Not to be hungry most of the time was another new experience for him!

Fast Forward!

Jose helped me in my Broadcast ministry, along with others, to operate the station transmitter. We were a non-commercial station, depending on assistance from volunteers.

In future years these are some of the things Jose did with his life: He eventually attended the same Bible College I graduated from. He also earned a BA degree in Political Science. He joined the Border Patrol agency, and that is the reason you do not know his last name.

Here is a summary, in his own words:

I'm currently a detective supervisor. I've had a variety of assignments during my career. Custody Patrol, and SWAT team. (I got to patrol the skies of Los Angeles during the '84 Olympics.) I transferred to Detective Headquarters and saw stints on the Child Abuse and homicide details. I *"leased"* my services to a Federal Taskforce, where I worked alongside FBI, ATF and DEA agents! *(He traveled a bit to other states also.)* I'm currently a supervisor at Detective Headquarters! "

Jose spent many years before retirement in the service of HIS COUNTRY...*THE U.S.A!* WOW.... Thank you, Jose! He also was married and has three fine, grown children!

Joni In San Diego

When I arrived in San Diego California to put KECR FM on the air, one of the first people I met was Joni Melsted. She was a secretary for Dr. Tim LaHay, a well known church pastor and writer of Christian Books.

Joni babysat the LaHay kids often, in addition to being the Secretary for the church. She was a very organized, dedicated young lady. Her passion in life was to teach and educate young people of all ages, especially those in their teen years. Her routine was to do her job at the church during daily working hours, then pick up teens from the community of El Cajon, by age group, and take them to her home. She taught the kids Bible Stories, Missionary stories, and let some of the teens become leaders in the group. Those in leadership roles thus grew in their personal confidence and abilities. Everything about her home studies had GROWTH factors planned by Joni.

When that session was ended, Joni then took that group home, loaded up her van with a second and older aged group, and gave them the same Biblical/Missionary materials she gave the first group. So Joni's evening classes didn't end until about 9pm. However, she also planned ahead to the next day's sessions, making her total day one very long, strenuous endeavor!

We Meet!

I was a new comer, and unbeknown to Joni and I, some people set out to make sure Joni and I met each other! "Somehow" I was invited to be a visitor to one of Joni's evening classes. I was very impressed that all she did was play the piano, while the young people conducted the entire meeting. (I should point out that Joni gave piano lessons to literally thousands of people of all ages, during her lifetime).

Story Telling!

One of Joni's gifts was to be able to develop a story in her mind at a moment's notice.
There was a time when one of her students raised his hand and asked, *"Miss Joni, tell us a story!"* So she told the story about Johnny's Lost Kite. He had just built a nice kite, complete with a tail, and was ready to fly it on a fairly windy day. When he let out the string a little at a time, everything went fine, until

suddenly a strong gust of wind snapped the string, and his beautiful kite went sailing off into the neighborhood. Johnny ran as fast as he could, keeping an eye on where it landed. Finally, he saw the kite being picked up by the neighborhood bully! The bully claimed it was HIS kite. *"Finders Keepers, Losers weepers!"* Johnny thought fast... *"I've got a quarter, I'll buy it from you!"* The Bully said, *"aahh..OK gimme ur ol' quarter!"* As Johnny walked away with his kite held tightly to his chest, he spoke to it, *"Little kite, now you are twice mine! First I Built you, then I bought you!"*

And Joni made the obvious application of God making each of us, then He died for us!

Marriage

Three pastors married Joni and I. My own pastor from Lakeside, California,
Derrick Johnson, a musician whom we both knew from Bible College, and Pastor Orval Butcher, of Skyline Wesleyan Methodist Church.

Having to give up her ministry with children was a difficult decision to make. However, joining me at KECR-FM Radio Station opened the door to broaden her outreach to adults! Joni not only became my Secretary at the station, but also helped in many ways for us to extend our programing. Family Radio Network in San Francisco provided over 95% of our listening fare. However, now we could produce some evening programs live, to reach for our El Cajon and San Diego listeners!

National Listeners

Joni's talent in telling stories was a natural gift! So the two of us began to produce a weekly show called *"Moments of Inspiration with Joni."* That 15-minute program not only was aired to our local audience, but to the entire Family Radio Network of the three west coast stations, but also to all of the other affiliate stations spread across much of the nation. She not only read stories, but poems and heart-warming thoughts. I remember one time when she was in the Production Room reading a story and I was in the Recording Booth. She had chosen a very emotional story, preceded by another reading, and did not fully realize the connection between the two readings until she read them aloud! It was such a Spirit-lead moment, that the two of us looked at one another with tears in our eyes at the impact it made!

The NARB!

Every January there is a meeting in Washington, D.C. called, "The National Association Of Religious Broadcasters." I attended one of those meetings, at which time I not only learned much about Christian radio and TV stations nationally, but also met many of the leaders including Pat Robertson, leader of CBN. Pat knew of my background in Television, and my interest in starting a TV Network on the west coast.

CBN was still in its infancy, operating out of what was called the Tide water. Pat asked if it might be possible for Family Radio to give me a six-month leave of absence to come back and be his Production Director.

Family Radio granted me six months, so Joni

and I packed up our belongings and drove across country to do that very thing.

CBN Network

Many people each day watch Pat Robertson and his staff at CHRISTIAN BROADCAST NETWORK. Today, I also watch that network often. It brings back memories of what those six months on loan from Family Radio Network entailed.

I have no desire to malign or put down Pat in even the slightest.

However, the day I walked into the studio of his station in the Tidewater area, I was amazed at how there was little organization. I had worked with more than one TV station on the west coast, and was used to absolute timing of each program, it's beginning, what commercials and inserts are adhered to, right down to the seconds.

The day I met my crew of mostly volunteers, and only a Chief Engineer, and Program Director, I was in for a shock. I asked for a Program Log and all I was given was a blank look from the staff. One person did some volunteering at a commercial station, so he alone knew what I meant. Later, he said, "You should have seen the look on your face when nobody knew what you asked for!"

Following that introduction, Pat was scheduled to do his usual 700 Club at 5:30pm.

The time came and Pat didn't show up. Meanwhile, nobody on the staff knew what to expect. Would he just stand behind a pulpit and begin to preach, or would he show up with a guest? If he had a guest, or several, would he need a piano for his guest to play? How many microphones would we need? All we could do as staff was to fill in Public Service announcements, or promotions of other programs. He had no concept of being on time, or preparation!

One of the next things I tackled was to broadcast nightly news. In Klamath Falls, Oregon, we used a rear screen projection system so Polaroid shots of news features would appear in the background. I did those newscasts personally until leaving CBN. Viewers today see that type of rear screen news in every CBN Broadcast.

Jim & Tammy Fay Bakker!

In the afternoon Jim and Tammy Fay Bakker, two former evangelists, put on a kids show. I can't remember how it went, accept that Tammy was a "very blond" blond, with an ego that didn't quit. Often, when Jim was talking to kids or an audience, Tammy would saunter and strut slowly across the background, so everyone in the audience would see her "Pretty Face."

Many people know the future events that were promoted by this couple, and the effect it had on Christian TV for years.

A Zoom Lens!

The second major acquisition I made was to purchase a used zoom lens from a TV studio. Prior to that, there was the obsolete three lens camera, where large group shots were only made with difficulty. It cost only about $100, and I was ecstatic to show how now, for the first time, a long shot of an entire chorus group could be aired, or if we so chose, just zoom in for a close-up on one person.

On the day before it was time to leave CBN and return to the west coast, I entered my office, to find long rolls of News info sheets taped all over my office. Staff had written loving comments such as, *"We'll miss you...have a safe trip...love you a bunch...etc."* I phoned home to Joni and told her with tears in my eyes what people had written! The night I left, I saw one of the young men standing outside the studio waving goodbye with tears in his eyes! So did I!

Long Trip Home

Joni was about 7 months pregnant with our first son. I had just turned 40 years old.
That weekend I sat under an Oak tree and pouted for hours. I thought to myself:
"Now I'm an old man! When my kid is 40, I'll be

60! That means we won't even be able to communicate, because there will be a generation gap between us!" What a pity party!

The long trip home was indeed LOOONG! Our doctor had limited us to only 200 miles a day! We did see some new sites, such as the Presidential Memorial, Mount Rushmore,0 etched into the mountains of South Dakota. Daytime temperatures were very hot, and Joni was bounced constantly. She was miserable! On our last day approaching Merced, California, we stretched our miles to nearly 400!

Joni delivered son Dan at the proper time. What changes that made in our lives!

Return to Klamath Basin

About 40 years ago I returned to the Klamath Basin with my young family, after having managed several Christian Radio Stations in California.

I had helped put KOTI-TV on the air many years earlier, in June of 1956. The new station manager, Don Stonehill, offered me a position selling TV time and programing.
However, now my heart really wasn't in commercial broadcasting, but in non-commercial Christian radio!

NO one in the Klamath Basin knew what it was like to hear Christian programing 24 hours a day. <u>That became my goal</u>!

The question was: How do we make it happen? The closest full time Christian FM station was KVIP FM in Redding, California.

Research

Normal AM or FM stations operate with thousands of watts. However, now the FCC had authorized a new system of low power Translators. 10 watts could be used with directionalized antennas and increased a few more watts to cover small towns and communities.

I contacted KVIP Directors, and we investigated possibilities. They flew up to Klamath Falls, and we sought mountain tops to place a local translator. Hamaker Mountain, where a Radar Site was operating, appeared to be a possibility, *IF* the Lord opened the right doors. First, I formed a Non Profit organization: Inspiration Radio Southern Oregon, in July of 1976, and established a Board of Directors. We also applied with the FCC for a Station Authorization.

Opposition!

Do you remember that years earlier in San Diego where I encountered what I called "Electronic Demons"? Delay is a tool our spiritual enemy often uses to his advantage.

Thus, approval of our Station Authorization by another operating radio station held up our application. However, the Lord had other plans in mind, and some attorneys I didn't even know existed, contacted the FCC on our behalf. The FCC staff felt the public interest was important, and saw no purpose in referring approval from the full seven commissioners. *Our station authorization was granted! PTL!*

Signal Path

There were several small communities in the 150-mile stretch between KVIP-FM in Redding. Most of the towns were located at the base of the tall mountains, and their Translator had to be near the top of a site. When heavy snow fell, their small building was often buried, and no signal could be picked up, nor relayed to the next small town.

Klamath Falls was always the last in line which needed a signal. No signal in one area meant no signal in our area. Thus there were several years of improvements needed to keep those stations on the air.

Quality? That was another problem! A symptom called temperature inversion and "Multi path" often would make the radio signal sound poor. Thus, even if the signal was on the air delivering KVIP to a town, the quality would be bad. So there was many a day when Klamath Falls had Christian radio, but I was downright embarrassed at the quality!

Team Mates

In broadcasting, there are two essential operative people who make it possible for a signal to be sent over the airwaves:

(1) Announcers, like myself, who think...

people!
(2) Engineers, who think electronics!
These people working together make a dedicated Team!

In our case, Roger Brown was our Chief Engineer. I cannot begin to tell you how much Roger was essential to Inspiration Radio Southern Oregon. I still remember the day our little Translator arrived in the mail. Roger and his wife Paula and I gathered together around that little box of electronics, laid hands on it, and prayed that God would use this man-made item to reach out and *change peoples hearts and lives!*

Roger's skills and dedication were called upon many, many times to repair and replace parts on our Translator, and return our programing to the airwaves. *Thank you Father for Roger!*

The Radar Site

In order for the Inspiration Radio Southern Oregon to bring the KVIP's signal to Klamath Falls, we needed the maximum elevation we could find. Hamaker Mountain was ideal at 6,552 feet above sea level, and was the site of a WW II military radar site. Even to this present day Hamaker is used for distant area coverage for specific tasks.

We were authorized by the FCC 34 years ago to put a 10-watt translator on a sloping side of the hill, below the radar equipment.

Snow was very often a major obstacle of whether or not we could drive the 9 miles to install, and maintain IRSO's Receiver/Translator! Many times I could not drive up the slippery grade, even with a donated 4-wheel drive Jeep. Sliding backwards with no traction is scary!

On the positive side, once we had our Translator operational, the unit was both a Receiver and a Transmitter, which did not require maintenance often. That meant our Board Members could maintain our jobs full time, and we were only called upon to drive to the hilltop for occasional repairs.

We planted a 20-foot telephone pole in the ground, which we climbed to install a Receiving Antenna to pick up KVIP. Below it we chained a refrigerator box to the pole, and put our small Translator/Transmit unit inside. We thought it would offer protection from external cold and winds. WRONG!

Have you ever tried to keep warm inside your car while sleeping in it at night without heat? The refrigerator coldness only popped the electronic circuit boards! Our solution? LOTS OF PRAYER!

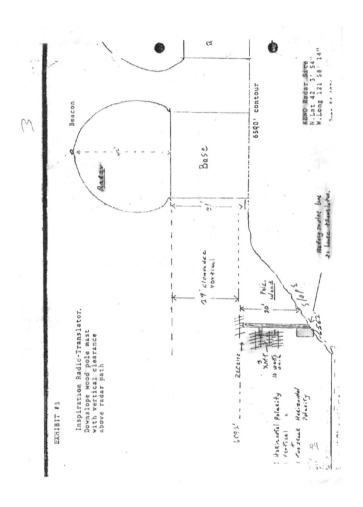

EXHIBIT #5

Inspiration Radio-Translator.
Downslope wood pole mast
with vertical clearance
above radar path

God Knew About it!

God had better things in mind all along! There was a rectangular shaped building nearby called "The Gator Building", Ground to Air Radio Building. This was used by Kingsley Field Air Training operations. Much of the space was no longer in use, and we were allowed to move our little Translator into a portion of it. There were very few restrictions. Free rent, no power bill... ever, for many years. Praise the Lord!

One day one of our Board Members named Bill Havlina asked if I'd ever heard of KLOVE Radio. (Bill recently graduated to Heaven.) KLOVE Radio was a real God send. We became close friends with their expanding radio ministry. In fact, we invited them to place an electronic rack of equipment 2 feet from ours. What a difference! We still were limited to 10 watts of power, while theirs was 140 watts of power, and operated from remote control from Central California.

In the winter time when snow made it difficult for us to get up to the hilltop, they owned a Snow Cat tractor, and they let me ride along with their technician. We traveled up the hill at 9 mph, and down at 29 mph! KLOVE now sends its radio stations around the world via satellite.

Fast Forward!

Haymaker Mountain at the Radar site was not the most ideal location for good coverage of the Klamath Basin. Another mountain closer to the city and suburbs of Klamath Falls would be much more ideal. Again, God knew this and KVIP was able to make a trade of locations and frequency with the CSN Calvary Network. That trade, in August of 2010, immediately brought a much stronger signal coverage to the Klamath area.

That much better signal thus allowed IRSO to go off the air entirely. We traded our frequency, and call sign to KLOVE Radio and we went completely off the air!

The events I have written about are all past history!
What more can I say? We at Inspiration Radio Southern Oregon were Pioneers in bringing the Gospel message, oh so slowly, using the only methods we knew about, to as many people as we could reach!

THANK YOU FATHER FOR ALLOWING US TO BE A SMALL PART OF YOUR PLAN!

OIT 23 Years

I had never expected to become a College Instructor, until Dr. Winston Purvine asked me to join the faculty. At the time of his request, I was still at KOTI-TV. But getting a higher paycheck was an incentive, so I accepted his offer.

As Public Relations Director, I handled all of the news reports to the local media. Part of that was to produce a weekly TV show called *"Tech Talks."* Normally I interviewed OIT faculty members, or even students, who had special talents. Eventually, I purchased our own TV camera, which made it possible to take that camera into a classroom and record a typical day or hour in class. It was something many people had never experienced before.

One day Dr. Purvine asked me to accompany him to the Airport to meet several Taiwanese Presidents who were interested in learning about Oregon Tech. As these men stepped off the plane, I greeted them in Chinese. Neither they nor Dr. Purvine expected my greeting. I was not really fluent in Mandarin, but knew enough to get by during my two years in China in 1947-49. At the next faculty meeting

Dr. Purvine told the faculty, "*You never know what hidden talents our faculty has. The other day I asked Bill Clark to join me at the airport to meet some men from the Far East. When Bill talked Chinese, it just tickled the Hell out of 'em.*"

Speech Instructor

Part of my duties were to teach Speech and Broadcasting. All students are required to take Speech classes in order to graduate. Most students dread to stand in front of a class and give a talk. In meeting a new class, the first thing I did was to turn to the blackboard and write in large letters, "**87%**" Then I would tell them, "*Class unless you deliberately tell us you are scared, 87% of your nervousness is <u>unnoticed</u>. By the end of this term, you will find that this class may be one of your favorite classes, and that we've all become one happy family!*"

A Summer fatality!

At the end of my first year at OIT, the students had all gone home for the summer. I left my office, started the car, and planned to drive around campus to the Motor Pool to pick up a State Vehicle. At that time, the road going around the south campus was only an unpaved dirt road. Driving along, I noticed a pickup truck on the left side of the road ahead, which was stopped. As I neared it, I could see the driver behind the wheel, pushing and fighting with his wife. Then as I came almost even with the pickup, her door flew open, and a pistol came flying out, landing on the ground! I think, *"Whoa, what's going on here?"* Then, somehow the male driver jumped out of her side, grabbed the pistol, stood up **put the pistol under his chin and pulled the trigger**! I couldn't believe what I just saw. I did a fast 180 degree turn around, dust still flying in the air from my car, and the man, still with pistol in his hand, was looking straight at me! Why? Was he going to keep on squeezing the trigger, maybe out of convulsion?

No time to worry about that right now, this guy will need some help fast! So I drove up to the nearby hospital as fast as I could to get an ambulance. Remember, there were no cell phones then. I had to drive to get help.

Meanwhile, there were two girls working on campus buildings who heard the shot, investigated, and phoned State Police. When I got back, he was still lying on the ground. There wasn't anything more I could do, but go back to my office and phone my wife Joni.

When she answered, I told her quietly and in shock, *"I just saw a man shoot himself!"* Several friends were with Joni, and she had to

quiet them down. *"What did you say?"*
I repeated my statement, and the women prayed.

God always has a Reason!

That night I couldn't get to sleep. I've always, always, believed that NOTHING ever happens to a Christian by accident. There always has to be a reason!

The next day I found out the man was not dead. The pistol bullet did not come up thru his brain, but rather at the base of his nose. One more inch toward his brain, and he would have died! Some weeks later I was able to contact the man, and be there to help the man put his life back together again! *Praise God for his plans and purposes!*

Moving On

In the years ahead, I was in for some disappointments and hurts. It was the first time I had worked in a large organization. Yes, there were Christian faculty and students, none of us were perfect. But the *"Dog eat Dog"* attitudes and life styles of faculty became very apparent.

Somebody always wanted my Job or someone else's job!

And they didn't care what tactics they used to try to get the position. I won't go into details now. I've just come to believe that no matter what job you have, even a restaurant waiter, someone wants your job! (Perhaps your job would bring you higher tips.)

There were marital problems among staff, and almost everyone knew about the infidelity that went on. Day after day, typical insecurity and unfaithfulness reigned.

Yet, there was never a day that I dreaded going to work. There were some faculty and students who were the salt of the earth, and I loved them.

Graduation Time

The end of each school year brought the many awards, recognitions and speeches that are normal in any graduation ceremony. One thing about College/University regalia is the many colored and unique robes of Faculty. Every professor's gowns are different and represent the level of rank earned from different universities. They all are beautiful and indicate our past achievements.

One of these days we will all graduate from this earth, and step into Eternity!

The robes our Father gives us at our Heavenly entry will be dazzling in color, meaning and honor! Robes of Splendor earned from Earthly service and devotion to our Risen Savior!

May we each hear and read His diploma He gives us:

"Welcome Home my child. Well done thou good and faithful servants!"

Amen!

A Major Look Back!

The title of this book shows three divisions of who I was and am! Sailor, Broadcaster, and Chaplain to inmates!

One Sunday morning in 1998 I was on route to church, and passed a building I never really paid much attention to before. It was called "Juvenile Detention Hall", and there were several boys outside raking leaves. All of them wore uniforms, and it caused me to wonder why? During the next week I felt as if the Lord wanted me to do some investigation into what was happening there.

The facility was for teenagers who had been in trouble with the law, and were being detained, often because of drugs. I knew very little about drugs (even as an ex-sailor), or many of the charges that these boys were being charged with. To my surprise, I was offered the opportunity to make Monday evening visits, get acquainted, and hold Bible Studies.

Here are some common factors each of the teens share:

(1) 70% of the boys either do not know who his dad was, or

(2) the father was dead, or

(3) the father was in Prison, or

(4) the folks split, and he *never had a role model* in his life.

Other factors: about 30% have ADD, ADHD, Bipolar or worse. Some take medications, while others do not. ADD can make it difficult for students in school to focus on studies. There is a tendency for those kids to seek out others who have a similar background, and may become involved with vandalism, smoking, alcohol, shoplifting thefts, pot, or these days with Meth. In short, there 's a hole in their heart! I tell them they *have a hole in their heart only Jesus can fill!*

Bear in mind that these are teens... many of whom end up in prison!

Our Beginnings!

During the time I began holding midweek services at Juvenile Hall, a house church on

Sunday mornings began to shape our future, unbeknown to us. Kent Barry, current Director of the Gospel Mission, led a group of about 18 adults and children in worship services. Someone in the group mentioned that a needy family in Sacramento California was planning to move to Klamath Falls. That person made the suggestion of how nice it would be if we as a group were to host a Christmas party for them. We all agreed, and decided to put the names of the children in a hat, and pass it around. When a name was drawn, we were to buy a Christmas gift for that kid. I drew the name of a 12-year-old boy named Tim. Because of cold weather, 1 bought a warm jacket for him.

Christmas came and went, and no Tim or family showed up. However, the name of that kid who I'd never met, bugged me night and day. I couldn't get him off my mind... and that scared me to pieces. I thought *"Why can't I get this kid off my mind? Am I gay or something?"*

What we didn't know was that the family did come to Klamath Falls, and Tim had an attack of appendicitis. In the hospital he was given medicine to which he was allergic, and *he was fighting for his life.* The Holy Spirit had put this boy on my mind for reasons I was not aware of. First, for his health, and secondly, Tim's background in drugs! He taught me things about our present society of which I had *no* understanding. I joined Kent Barry, his family, and house church associates for over two years of fellowship, summer camp programs in Mountain Resorts, and for my own growth and experience.

"Promise Keepers"

One summer a national program swept the country to make men accountable to themselves and to their sons for deep Spiritual commitment! We heard renown speakers who pointed out areas which needed to be changed within our families. Sexual temptations and shortcomings was often one of the topics addressed. These meetings were held in football fields and community stadiums. Tim Williams and other young men we had been working with were in the groups who attended those conferences. For two years, God made *Promise Keepers* life changing!

Incorporation

I soon realized that asking other people to join me would result in a greater outreach to troubled youth. So on November 15, 1999 the Oregon State Corporations Division granted our request to become a Religious and

Charitable Corporations, organized and operated for religious, charitable and educational purposes exclusively.

Our bylaws and Articles of Incorporation listed three people initially, and we added two others later. I was designated as Director and Chaplain. However, we actually began our outreach over much of the state of Oregon three years later. We made visits to a number of conferences, Youth Ranches, Hillcrest (which at that time was for girls), and McLaren School for boys.

Behavioral Modification

Our Court system normally sentences youths to change their thinking, attitudes, and lifestyle! The youth's age, number of times he or she is sent to Juvenile Hall, and the reason why they were arrested is the basis for sentencing decisions.

A teen is required to meet a County Judge, who normally sentences him to out-of area treatment in group facilities. Some of the kids change their thinking and learn, while others run away (if it is not a lockup). If a youth continues to fail treatment, he may be sentenced to the Oregon Youth Authority. OYA then takes charge until he or she is 25 years old if necessary.

There were several of those sites within a few miles of Klamath Falls, and I began to visit them and understand their Leaders program to teach responsibility. Typical days meant go to school for 2 hours, work in the woods chopping trees, and then after lunch, reverse the process. Working alone gave the boys time to reflect on where he was going in life. Staff evaluated him at the end of each week on his attitude, cooperation, learning, etc. If at the end of several weeks he showed improvement, then he was permitted a weekend visit with parents. After a home visit he was given a UA (Urinalysis Analysis.) UA's are still a requirement for almost every offender, with unscheduled exams.

MacLaren Visits

I was still not interested in Adult Prisons, but I did learn about MacLaren School for Boys in Woodburn, Oregon. It was one of the oldest Rehab centers in the State, and did not even have a high fence around it. Working with their Chaplain, I began to make periodic visits to become acquainted with young men, and learn how they were schooled. This was a few years after I had been with Sermons From Science, and was able to speak to several large groups about science and the Bible. After one of those speaking engagements, it was an honor to have many young men line up and shake my hand.

Getting to Know Teens!

Early on, I determined NOT to start preaching to a Juvenile offender. My goal has always been to find out who he IS, and why! A special form helps me to reach that goal.

That form is worth its weight in gold. During Thursday morning visitation at Juvenile Hall, this Q&A form answers my questions, and also lets the kid get to know me, as well.

In about a dozen years, I've kept records on at least 1,000 youth. It helps me to keep track of how often he returns, what facility he has been sent to, and his progress or lack of growth.

Visit Prisons?

Prisons, you're kidding! Ever since I started working with teens in Juvenile Hall, there was no interest on my part about having anything to do with adult prison inmates. *No way Jose!*

But God had other plans!

My good friend John Karaglou suggested we take three boys on a visit to Pelican Bay in Crescent City, California in February 2003. We were to visit what was called by prisoners,

"The Rock Program!" ROCK meant: Reaching Out... Convicts to Kids! The programs goal was to help at-risk youths by opening their eyes to what lies ahead for them if they don't make changes in their lives!

Inside Greetings!

We arrived on a sunny morning, and were greeted by inmates who told us, "Prison isn't a nice place to live. There are no birds, no animals to play with, and no friendly faces to make you feel happy. You wouldn't like being here. While you're here we expect you to treat us with respect and do everything we tell you!" (Note: Respect is what inmates have lost in life, and in prison they demand it!)

For the next seven hours we were educated about prison life. We saw videos of fights and treachery. About a half dozen inmates introduced themselves, telling how they'd killed people, about losing their children and family, and in some cases were in tears as they spoke.

Next was a visit to a cell. Prior to the visit, each boy had filled out an application which told about his family life and about the behavioral problems he had at home. Each of the inmates had read those forms and were ready to pounce in the kids face.

Taken to a 6x9 prison cell their accusations hit home. *"This is where we live, Boy! If y'all don't straighten out yo' life , you gonna live jus' like this, Punk!"* The boy gets tears in his eyes. *"You can't cry in prison. In here if you got tears in yo eyes, we gonna git yo ass!"* Another inmate chimes in. *"An when he gits done with ya, I'm gonna git sum!"*

The Yard

Before we were allowed in the exercise yard, we were told by a female guard that should we be taken hostage by inmates, there will be no negotiations for your release! (*Gulp*)!

Thankfully, we had 4 female guards and 2 male guards with us at all times. Inside we saw several guard towers as we passed through two outer fences. However, between those 2 fences was an inner wire carrying deadly high voltage. Our guide officer explained that some inmates were sex offenders, and should any of them whistle at our boys, just ignore them. Sure enough, a very dark black prisoner with huge false boobs sidled up close to our boys and said, *"Heeey Guys, Come up to maah scell,*

&ah 'll show ya'all what a real man is liiike!" I thought our boys were gonna heave!

Warnings

We were also warned that if you hear loud speakers come on, and you see inmates dropping to the ground, move to the nearest wall and don't move!

It Happened!

A loud speaker came on, and inmates dropped. So did we! Up ahead about 50 yards there had been a stabbing. One dark inmate had walked through a group of others, slashed the throat of another inmate, and disappeared back into his group. The wounded inmate clasped his throat, then began running and guards threw towels around his neck. There was an immediate strip search of inmates in that area, and when we moved into that area we saw a pool of blood. We assumed he died, but days later we found out he lived.

It's all on Video Tape!

In God's mysterious ways, a TV News reporter had accompanied us, and he took footage of the tour and how sincere inmates attempted to convince the 3 boys, *"This is prison life, boy!*

This is reality! You don't want to come to this place!"

We also saw videos of riots in the prison. Just another normal day on the inside!

Three Days Later!

Only three days after we left Pelican Bay, a big riot happened on B Yard. 12 inmates were injured and several killed. It was of such magnitude that media across the United States reported the events. Since we had just visited Pelican Bay, the local newspaper, radio and television stations interviewed John Karaglou, the St. Claire boy I had taken on the trip, and myself.

After that riot every inmate was restricted to life inside the building for two years. NO one was allowed yard privileges. Life at Pelican Bay has never been the same!

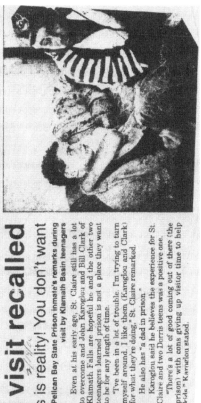

Violent prison visit recalled

'This is prison life, boy! This is reality! You don't want to come to this place!'

— A Pelican Bay State Prison inmate's remarks during visit by Klamath Basin teenagers

By DOUG HIGGS
H&N Staff Writer

An inmate got stabbed.

Several guards were held hostage.

And there were lots of fences, some with high voltage that's deadly, to keep cons inside.

These are just some of the things 15-year-old Dustin St. Claire of Klamath Falls remembers about his visit with two other teenagers and two adults to Pelican Bay State Prison near Crescent City, Calif., last Saturday. The prison was rocked with a violent riot this week, which

Even at his early age, St. Claire still has a lot to overcome and John Karoglou and Bill Clark of Klamath Falls are hopeful he and the other two teenagers learned prison is not a place they want to be for any length of time.

"I've been in a lot of trouble. I'm trying to turn myself around. I like them (Karoglou and Clark) for what they're doing," St. Claire remarked.

He also has "a dad in prison."

Karoglou said he believes the experience for St. Claire and two Dorris teens was a positive one.

"There's a lot of good coming out of there (the prison) with cons giving up visitor time to help kids," Karoglou stated.

Summary
Past & Present Inmate History

In our early years of visiting prisoners, it was necessary for me to drive thousands of miles in Oregon, plus visiting many prisons in California. Time and expenses were major factors, not to mention the fatigue!

Today, letters and phone calls have reduced those tiring miles.

Writing an increasing number of letters did payoff in showing my devotion and concern for each person, in addition to understanding their present living conditions.

As an example, one woman inmate I've known for sometime was recently attacked and almost killed by two other women. She was knocked down and the women jumped up and down on her back. Even today my friend is experiencing physical difficulties and anger!

Another series of letters included a long time relationship with a man who wanted to commit suicide. He waited one morning for his cellmate to leave for the yard, then slashed his own throat. God apparently changed the mind of his cellmate to return early and he was able to call for the medics. Several years later, that same man tried another suicide attempt. This time a Nurse "happened" to find him with his throat slit. Today, that good friend of mine is walking much closer to the Lord, and may soon be released from prison altogether!

Accepting collect telephone calls is now an integral and welcome part of touching both men and women inmates lives! From their standpoint a caring voice shuts out the persistent noisy surroundings they are sentenced to hear 24 hours a day! From my end, I can sense almost at once how he or she feels at the moment. Dollars and cents from a collect call are insignificant!

Book Store Distribution

In recent months, our Lord has opened the door for multiplying the outreach of our prison ministry tremendously! *"For His Glory Bookstore"* has partnered with us to send Bibles and a variety of Christian literature to every one of the 14 prisons in Oregon and others!

Many of the books are true stories of Christian athletes, explorers, pilots and world travellers. Every prison houses inmates who are lost, lonely and just plain bored. Amazing stories not only encourage the inmate, but often prompt him or her to reach out to cellmates to take a stand for the Lord!

I know of one man who in his early trouble making days was a genius at encouraging other teens to join him in destroying property or the generosity of adult caregivers. Now after serving many years in lockup, he is down to only a few years before being released. He is like a son to me, and like several other inmates, he calls me "dad." In his present facility God has called him to reach out to other inmates and he takes a real stand for Christ! Now almost daily, while walking "the yard" an inmate will stop him and ask questions. He then gives me the name and prison sid#. Not only do I write that person, but also my Bible Bookstore owner then sends a list of good Christian reading material, and we seek to help that inmate learn and grow spiritually!

It is apparent that God has a major plan for this young man's life, which will give him direction and purpose in life!

How about you?

Let me give you a Bible verse to memorize and guide your path:

Jeremiah 29:11 says, *"For I know the plans I have for you, says the Lord! They are plans of good and not for evil... to give you a hope and a future."*

Take Him up on it... You won't be sorry!!!

From left to right: my son Dave Clark/Fire Chief, son Dan Clark/Audio Video Interiors, son Bob Clark, and me-Bill Clark/88 year old Author and Chaplain.

Resume in Brief

Bill Clark
Juvenile Detention & Prison Ministries
3939 So. 6ᵗʰ Street #255
Klamath Falls, OR 97603

Military: US Navy Radio Operator 1945~'49
            2 years in Philippines & 2 in China

Education: AA degree Speech & Radio
            BA Theology Pacific Bible College
            MA Television Production

Broadcasting:
            -Career in commercial and Christian
            Radio & Television stations.
            -Announcer, Salesman, Production

Director, News Director

-5 year star of Captain Uncle Bill show (Daily kids' outer space show)

-Production Director of Pat Robertson's 700 Club

-Manager of Christian FM stations in San Diego & Merced California

-President of Inspiration Radio Southern Oregon, bringing KVIP & KLOVE Christian Radio stations to Klamath Falls.

College Teaching:

-23 years at Oregon Institute of Technology as Associate Professor (Speech & Broadcasting)

-Director of Publications & Information, Financial Aids Counselor.

Ministries:

-Founding member of Klamath Falls, Gospel Mission.

-Member of various Mission Boards, Tijuana, Mexico, US Church Boards &

-KLEOS children's Ministry

-Special calling: Director of Juvenile Detention & Prison Ministries.

-Over 15 years mentoring teens. Pen Pal & visitor to Prisoners in Oregon, California.

-CASA Volunteer (Court Appointed Special Advocate) to Children.

-Writer and Story Teller.